reclaim

reclaim

HOW TO STOP SCROLLING THROUGH YOUR LIFE AND START LIVING IT

HEATHER HENDERSON

Cover Illustration: Heather Henderson
Cover & Layout Design: Ian Koviak, The Book Designers

Published by Fernlight Books
San Francisco, California
www.fernlightbooks.com

Library of Congress Control Number: 2026913614
ISBN: 979-8-996161-91-1 (paperback)
ISBN: 979-8-996161-92-8 (hardcover)

To the women who inspired me,
the students who taught me,
and the lovers who helped me grow.

CONTENTS

AUTHOR'S NOTE

In March 2026, as this book was going to print, juries in California and New Mexico found Meta and Google negligent. Not for what people posted on their platforms, but for how the platforms were built. The jury concluded that the apps were designed to be addictive, that the companies knew, and that the design itself caused harm.

This book was written before those verdicts. But the question at its center has always been the same one this jury was asked to consider: Was this chosen for you, or did you choose it?

You were never the problem.

INTRODUCTION

"I've been feeling so depressed at home, and I thought I'd come here and feel something... Is everything boring? There must have been a time when the world had more mystery."

I've never felt more seen by something a character said than when I heard Portia say this line in season two of *HBO's White Lotus*. It didn't just resonate—it cut through the noise. It captures a feeling so many of us are too afraid to name.

She goes on: *"You come somewhere like this and it's beautiful, and you take a picture and realize everyone's taken the same picture from the same spot. You just made some redundant content for stupid Instagram."*

Even beauty starts to feel algorithmic.

And when she sighs and says, finally, *"You can't even get lost anymore because you can just find yourself on Google Maps,"* it landed with a heartbreak I didn't expect.

She wasn't talking about Sicily. She was talking about all of us—the way wonder has been replaced by repetition, how novelty has been replaced by documentation, and how even escape no longer feels like escape.

It was a brutal honesty I'd never heard articulated, not aloud. Because that is how it feels, right? To travel somewhere beautiful, hoping to feel something, to crave wonder or mystery or aliveness, and instead feel flattened by the fact that everything has already been posted, filtered, geotagged, and consumed.

I could feel her restlessness in my own body when she tells Albie: *"I'm sick of fucking TikTok and Bumble and screens and apps... I just wanna live my life so badly."*

This isn't just a rant. She voices what so many of us are terrified to admit: that even when we escape, we're not escaping. We're documenting. We're performing. We're producing content instead of feeling our lives.

We *should* feel more, we tell ourselves, but somehow don't. We're surrounded by beauty, yet disconnected from it.

In truth, beauty has become something to capture rather than inhabit or experience, and burnout stems from having too much of everything except the one thing we need: meaning. It's the sound of a generation exhausted by constant stimulation. The hollow ache of people surrounded by everything and somehow feeling nothing.

We laugh because it's familiar. We've all felt that quiet panic of wanting life to feel bigger, fuller, more alive, instead of this chronic sameness.

Portia isn't begging for a digital detox. She's begging for the part of life we traded away when we decided convenience mattered more than wonder.

Even our escapist TV has stopped pretending we're okay. The fantasy isn't wealth or luxury anymore—it's presence. And this is where the fiction dissolves into something painfully true. Off screen, the same story plays out everywhere. At the Four Seasons in Maui, guests sit inches from the Pacific, scrolling through beaches they're not looking at. On the double-decker Google bus in San Francisco, thousands ride in silence, faces lit by the blue glow of the very platforms they're paid to build.

In restaurants and cafés, people lift their phones to capture moments they're too distracted to feel. From the outside, it looks like a dream. From the inside, it feels like disconnection dressed up as modern life. What Portia names on screen is the same thing I'd been living off screen. Not just emotionally, but professionally.

As someone who spent a decade inside the companies that shaped the very world we're all trying to navigate, I know that feeling more intimately than most.

I hadn't even unpacked. Two days after moving to Austin for my first Fortune 500 recruiting job, I was already on a plane to Miami. When I walked into Visa's LATAM office and saw *Everywhere you want to be* on the giant digital displays, something lit up in me: Pride. For the first time, I was part of something with global impact. It wasn't just a tagline, either. It was a worldview. And I believed completely that technology was opening the world, one frictionless payment at a time. I didn't question what we might be losing in the process. I was too busy believing in it.

At Google, I remember sitting in an all-hands meeting and being handed a cookie with the phrase *Build for Everyone* iced on it. I felt powerful just holding it. No irony, no hesitation—just the quiet confidence of a brand trusted by the whole world. If we continued to build, everyone would benefit.

But "everyone" eventually became "everything." Every thought. Every click. Every moment logged in service of personalization. I didn't stop to ask who "everyone" excluded, or what it meant to optimize every moment.

Uber was different—again. It had edge. It was competitive, unapologetic, and it knew exactly what it was. When I'd see

Power of the Platform on campus giveaways, I felt it—that electric certainty that we were at the top and moving fast. The platforms weren't just connecting us anymore; they were defining us, shaping behavior, attention, even identity.

If I look back at the branded T-shirts, notebooks, and lanyards I've collected over the years, they read almost like cultural time stamps—markers of where we were and what we believed technology could do for us. *Everywhere you want to be. Build for Everyone. The Power of the Platform.* Three taglines. Three worldviews. Three versions of a promise I believed completely until I couldn't anymore.

My story didn't start in Silicon Valley. It started in a Barnes & Noble at Perkins Rowe in Baton Rouge, Louisiana, in the summer of 2009.

Perkins Rowe is one of those prefab downtowns that could be anywhere in America—the kind of place designed to feel like somewhere else: familiar enough to feel safe, generic enough to disappear into.

I was twenty-three, and my mom had just closed the Bank of Mom. Officially, lovingly, finally.

I was living with a guy I knew from high school, an underwater welder who loaded up the Isuzu Trooper and went offshore for days at a time—no service, no signal. Just sporadic emails and grocery lists for the quick visits home. My stay wasn't a free vacation. It was an olive branch at a moment that mattered.

Were we dating? Were we just friends? I couldn't tell you and, honestly, I didn't ask. You don't interrogate the life raft when you're drowning. The condition was quiet and unspoken, but real. Staying meant actively looking. Working on my resumé. Showing up for myself.

I felt like I was on an island. Five years of college had ended and suddenly there were no guardrails—no syllabus, no roommates, no structure that told you what came next. Just Louisiana, which for a California kid felt like an unknown world. The only thing that resembled home was Whole Foods Market. The brands that lined the aisles. The familiar smell of fresh food and expensive cheese. I'd shop for groceries and stay a little longer than I needed, just to quiet my homesickness.

I'd watch the neighbors living the house-mouse life and feel something close to admiration—I genuinely didn't know how they did it all. But I'd also watched women I loved build their lives around someone else's ambitions, their own dreams quietly set aside. I understood both. I just knew which one I was.

I left home at seventeen and never looked back. I had a degree in human development and one specific obsession: the moment young people have to figure out who they are without a syllabus telling them. But first I had to survive my own version of it.

I'd go to Barnes & Noble and sit on the floor in the career section; this was 2009, before you could just take a photo of your resumé and upload it into a bot. I went multiple times a week. Sometimes for the whole afternoon. Not because I had somewhere to be, but because it *gave* me somewhere to be.

The career section became my office. The floor became my desk. I'd pull books off the shelf and copy resumé formats and read interview guides and take notes on industries I knew nothing about. Nobody asked me to leave. Nobody noticed me. I was just a girl on the floor with a pen and whatever paper she had, figuring out how to get into rooms she'd never been in.

For the first time since graduation, I felt ready. Not certain. Not confident. Just ready—like if I kept showing up, the jobs would come back, and I'd be there when they did.

I became obsessed with resumés, which landed me my first job as an academic advisor. Which led to campus recruiting. Which led to Visa, Google, and Uber.

Which led here.

I didn't call it resourceful. I didn't call it anything. I just needed a job, and this was how you got one, so I showed up.

Fifteen years later, I had spent a decade inside the companies I'd once sat on the floor trying to reach.

Each company felt different. Each mission made sense. Looking back, the pattern is clear. We weren't just building tools that made life easier. We were building systems that decide what gets our attention and what gets left behind.

What none of us realized was that the convenience we were celebrating was also training us to expect instant access, to see any friction as failure. That life should always expand, never pause. That "everywhere" was the goal, and that slowing down was only for people lacking ambition.

I didn't study philosophy. I stumbled into it. I took Intro to Logic as a general education requirement, had a quiet moment of *whoa*, got a solid B, and moved on.

After graduation, I landed a job at UC Santa Cruz, advising two hundred philosophy students and the undergraduate club, the Philosophical Slug Society. I was twenty-four and one of the youngest academic advisors in campus history. I spent the next two years getting an informal education I'd never planned for.

I dated a graduate student—worn black leather jacket, tattoos, a devilish smile, and long brown hair the same length as mine. His studio was across the parking lot from the boardwalk. Stucco walls, red-tile roof, close enough that the screams from the Giant Dipper ride drifted in through the windows, along with the salty sea air.

He had a deep voice, raspy at the edges. He was finishing his dissertation, and I was trying very hard not to fall for him, which becomes impossible the moment someone sits across from you at golden hour and starts reading their work out loud.

He was writing about Martin Heidegger. I didn't understand all of it. But I understood the center of it—the idea that modern technology doesn't just change what we do. It changes how we see everything, ourselves included.

Occasionally, he'd look up between paragraphs to check that I was still there. I was always still there. And sometimes, almost offhandedly, he'd say something that felt less like dissertation material and more like a warning: The danger wasn't what technology could do. It was what it would quietly ask you to become.

I fell for him and, somewhere in that mix, for philosophy too. I carried those ideas with me without knowing it. I had no idea I was about to spend a decade inside the exact thing he'd been warning me about.

A few years later, I traded the redwoods for a recruiting desk. The philosophy students became engineering candidates. The boardwalk became campus travel.

Most mornings looked the same. Shower, Rag & Bone skinny jeans, Rothy flats, a work top. Then a quick coffee while getting dressed, a fifteen-minute drive to the shuttle stop in the dark, and the long ride south into Silicon Valley. I'd leave in darkness and often return in that same darkness, watching the world blur past the window as we fought our way north to the calm of Marin County.

It wasn't until I found myself on a bus full of brilliant, exhausted people, their heads bent over screens, that the words of that grad student I dated years earlier finally, truly landed.

That's where this book began—not as pages on a screen, but on that bus, staring out the window at a city full of people who had everything except the ability to be where they were. No one looked up. Outside, the city blurred past, and being present had become a luxury no one could afford.

Reclaim started as a whisper, a quiet knowing.

Somewhere along 19th Avenue, it hit me: I wasn't just living in this culture. I was helping to build it, and I no longer wanted to.

Between the campus info sessions and the offer calls, I started hosting workshops on imposter syndrome and well-being for students I would never be able to hire. I could only hire maybe 1 percent of the people in the room, but I wanted to show up for all of them. That distinction changed how I saw my work and, eventually, how I viewed the world.

The students taught me more than I'd expected. Some deleted TikTok during finals not as a productivity hack, but because the quiet made them feel human again. Others built phone-free study spaces or turned their rooms into intentional zones of focus. They were not waiting for someone to fix the attention economy. They were opting out of the parts that had cost them the most.

I saw it in the Uber intern classes too. A generation redefining what ambition looks like, asking for clear boundaries. They turned off Slack after hours so they could genuinely disconnect to live, refusing to perform busyness as a measure of worth. These were not acts of laziness. They were acts of clarity.

These students were not waiting for platforms to change. They were changing what they gave platforms access to: their time, their attention, their nervous systems.

That is when it finally clicked for me. Attention isn't just something we lose in small, forgettable ways. It is something we can direct, and the moment we choose where it goes, it becomes power.

I'm a four-time burnout survivor. Every company, every promotion, every so-called dream job ended the same way: with me exhausted and wondering how I had gotten there again. At some point, I had to face the pattern.

I had read the books. James Clear on atomic changes. BJ Fogg on tiny behaviors. Nir Eyal on how the hook was built and how to unhook yourself. I wasn't guessing. I knew what to do: Turn off notifications. Put your phone in another room. Create friction. Build better habits. And for a while, I did it. I would put my phone face down. Close the apps. Tell myself I was going to focus.

Then, without thinking, I would reach for it again. Not because I forgot, but because something in me still wanted—needed—something. Until I understood that no surface change was going to stick.

I was a self-proclaimed wellness enthusiast. A smoothie-loving, elimination-diet-obsessed, Peloton-riding tech recruiter. I sometimes took baths twice a day and listened to endless wellness podcasts, all in the name of "work-life balance." Yet I was one unsweetened oat-milk matcha latte away from completely losing it.

And while I'd subscribed to the sparkle of Instagram's wellness community, my true mindfulness journey began in 2019, when I registered solo for a book club at a local yoga studio. The book that month was Sharon Salzberg's *Real Happiness.*

It was a rainy, candlelit night. Here, in a circle of women I didn't know, something I had been outrunning finally caught up with me. Salzberg wrote, *"What arises in our experience is much less important than how we relate to what arises."* And if I didn't stop and tell the truth, I'd lose more than time or attention. I'd lose myself.

So I stopped. I stepped back. And started choosing differently.

Sometimes, that looks productive. Sometimes it's just staring at the ceiling calmly as I organize my thoughts without distraction. It's calmer. More importantly, though, it's mine. And, yes, some days I cave because I need distraction. I don't pretend that doesn't happen.

But even on those days, I can feel the difference.

My attention, my relationships, my ambition, my inner dialogue—they've all shifted. I can ask myself: *Did I choose this?*

Once choice returned, I returned to my life.

Instead of reaching for my phone first thing in the morning, I started sitting with my thoughts before my feet even touched the ground. I picked up Brianna Wiest's *The Pivot Year* and read it the way it was meant to be read: one day at a time, no skipping ahead. Then came the coffee, unhurried and uninterrupted. I took long walks and noticed, maybe for the first time in years, that spring smells like something. I took baths by candlelight with no podcast, no playlist, nothing to buffer the silence. Just the sound of water and the flicker of a flame.

But the thing that surprised me most was what happened in conversations. When you stop anticipating a notification, when your phone is just a phone and not a pulse you're constantly checking, you see people. You remember what they told you last week. You watch them light up when they realize you *were* listening the whole time. That is its own kind of gift.

I returned to the little girl who used to dream in the quiet. Who took in the world around her without cataloging it, without performing it. Who loved *living*, without worrying about what she was missing.

This book is my attempt to make sense of the world I helped create, and the world we're all trying to navigate. It's a guide for anyone who has ever felt Portia's ache, the disorientation of modern life, the sense that you've been scrolling through your own existence instead of living it.

Reclaiming yourself is not about rejecting technology. It is about remembering that you are the one who decides how you relate to it. For a long time, I treated these quiet returns to myself as private things, small rebellions in a world that had normalized distraction. But they were signs of something bigger—and I wasn't the only one looking for a way back.

The more people I talked to, the more I heard the same thing: exhaustion, overwhelm, and a sense that something important had gone missing.

This book isn't about escaping technology. It's about reclaiming your attention within it.

I spent years inside the systems that shaped modern digital life. I was the person checking my phone before my eyes were fully open—scrolling headlines before I'd said a word to myself. And I helped build the very thing I was trying to escape. But one decision led to another, and another.

The changes that followed weren't dramatic. They were specific. I spoke at UC Berkeley, at Michigan, and at Uber's intern cohorts without posting a single photo—and discovered the impact landed harder when I stopped performing it. I walked into SXSW EDU and chose presence over documentation. And slowly I stopped feeling guilty for not engaging with everything asking for my attention, and started noticing how much of it was missing the point.

This book is built around a simple truth I had to learn the hard way—one that changed everything once I finally saw it.

We don't reach for our phones because we're weak or distracted or addicted. We reach for them because we're human. Most of what drives our digital behavior comes down to five very human needs: ease, distraction, connection, growth, and impact. Not weaknesses. Not failures. Just needs.

And here's the thing: Tech meets them. Perfectly. Instantly. Every time.

That's the trap. It works, just not in a way that lasts or nourishes you or leaves you feeling more like yourself.

You'll start to recognize yourself in the patterns. The one who scrolls headlines before coffee not out of curiosity, but to brace. The one who stares at *Delivered*, trying to manage uncertainty through a text thread. The one who posts a win, then spends the next hour reading into who didn't like it. Each pattern has its own logic. Its own unmet need underneath. Its own way back.

That awareness is where this book lives. Not in the rules. Not in the restrictions. In the moment you remember that you're the one holding the device.

Reclaim is not a rejection of technology. It's a return to humanity. A reminder that we're still allowed to look up. Still allowed to feel. Still allowed to be here. You didn't lose yourself. You just forgot you had a choice.

part i

the problem

LOGGED ON + SILENT

My Cabo journey didn't start with a suitcase. It started with a scroll.

Cabo San Lucas is an influencer's paradise, with miles of white sand shoreline and rock formations that shoot straight out of gorgeous, turquoise-blue water. It's truly one of the most magical spots. The arch sits on the tip of the Baja Peninsula, where the Sea of Cortez meets the Pacific Ocean and where every sunset is a spectacle.

No wonder that it's become a top destination for those looking for a picture-perfect backdrop for their FOMO-inducing posts.

The very first Cabo post I ever saw was a proposal on a boat. I vividly remember Rachel's green silk dress as she stood on the bow of the vessel while her boyfriend, Bridger, whom she met in high school up in Lake Tapps, Washington, got down on one wobbly knee and proposed. It was gorgeous. I couldn't help but be in awe of the magical three-story-high landmark El Arco, even as I worried he might accidentally drop the ring. But he didn't, and she said yes.

A few months later, the lovely bride and groom were married in a beautiful sunset ceremony at The Cape, A Thompson Hotel in Cabo San Lucas. It was breathtaking. Now, if it sounds like I know these people, I do not. So if what I say next sounds crazy, I understand.

Within a week of watching the wedding, wishing I could step through the screen, I booked a weeklong stay for more than I'd ever paid for a hotel room. I didn't grow up taking trips like this. I was raised by a stepfather who was a mechanic and a secretary mother. More KOA campgrounds than STK Steakhouses. Summers on the river, not the Mexican Riviera.

I didn't dare tell my partner, Sean, why I chose the location. He hated influencers with a passion only reserved for anchovies and the 1-800 Kars-for-Kids commercial.

However, after years of following wellness influencer @Rachel-GoodEats and her bestie, @ShutTheKaleUp, I had come to trust them wholeheartedly. What started as simple meal prep posts, over years turned into sunset snaps that had me shelling out thousands.

Fast forward a few months, and we're on our influencer-inspired trip. I was loving it, and the hotel was stunning, the coffee otherworldly.

I stepped into the open-air lobby and stopped. It was one of the most impressive sights I've ever seen, with a direct view of the famous arch. The hotel seemed to float over the water, effortlessly playing on the natural beauty of the region and capturing the heart of every influencer in sight.

Yet something was off: The people at the pool were more interested in scrolling through their phones than engaging with others, and each sunset was more about creating content than truly experiencing the moment.

Standing at the top of the large spiral staircase, I watched person after person descend with their phones out, their backs turned to the sea. It felt as if we were trespassing in people's illusions, photobombing every time we tried to make our way down.

I wondered if I was missing the moment by not posting. By not getting the sunset dress photo.

THE OPEN-TAB MIND

These days, our lives feel more like an unwinnable game of mental Tetris. Clear one email, and three pop up. No matter how hard we try, the notifications keep stacking.

Right now, I have thirty-three tabs open on my laptop. *Thirty-three.* And that's not a metaphor—it's my actual browser. But it might as well be my brain.

Our minds jump from thought to thought, mentally everywhere yet emotionally nowhere. We're so sucked into our phones that we can't remember the last time we looked up, let alone what we just scrolled past.

I tried turning off notifications, only to wind up checking my phone more often. It was a feeling reminiscent of the yo-yo diet culture of the early 2000s, where Special K was sold as the "answer" even though it only left us hungrier. This isn't distraction. It's deeper. We're fragmented, overstimulated, and always somewhere else. And the people who built these systems don't use them the way we do. That's what I couldn't ignore.

Jack Dorsey—the co-founder of Twitter, a platform designed around constant updates and real-time attention—now practices some of the most extreme digital boundaries I've ever heard of.

I had two immediate reactions to Dorsey's boundaries. *One, that's insane. And two—of course. That makes total sense.* Because why would someone need monk-level discipline unless they'd built something so compelling that it required monk-level discipline to resist?

At the airport, I refreshed my gate info, checked texts, and scrolled on repeat. I was supposed to journal, but I got distracted by the buzz of a notification. I got lost in the scroll, only half hearing my boarding call. Twenty minutes later, I was settled into my seat and still hadn't pulled out my notebook, and my phone hadn't left my palm.

Here's the thing: It wasn't just me. And it isn't just airports. Digital distraction has seeped into every aspect of our lives. It's in classrooms, boardrooms, even the conference rooms of the most innovative companies in the world.

I was sitting across from a hiring manager in Chicago when my phone started losing its mind. Texts. Skype notifications. Emails stacking up.

My phone wouldn't stop. The hiring manager kept talking about the slides, but all I could feel was the pulse of every ping, each one a tiny jolt of adrenaline, a demand I couldn't escape. That's when I knew my relationship with technology had quietly broken.

It hadn't always been this way. In Santa Cruz, my phone was a tool for joy—group texts to plan weekday sailing trips or family dinners at Rancho Relaxo, our beach-adjacent hacienda complete with a tiki hut and hammocks perfectly positioned between the boardwalk and harbor. We were young professionals who loved doing cool things, and our phones helped us organize the fun. Once I was with people, I was there—phone away, present, part of the conversation as we watched the sunset over the wharf from the cliffs. Technology connected us to life, instead of pulling us away from it.

But then I moved to Austin to work in corporate. And suddenly the group texts weren't about connecting when we were apart. They were about proving you were always available, always responsive, always *on*. Every ping felt loaded. Every notification kept me alert, guarded, never relaxing long enough to be caught off guard. I went from open and excited to worn and drained.

It didn't start on my couch. It started in Stevenson Hall.

Senior year at Sonoma State. Student assistant in the provost's office. Concrete walls. Paper files stacked floor to ceiling. One chair in the waiting area directly in front of my desk. Not a lobby. Not a waiting room. Just a chair. Where faculty sat. Where administrators settled in. Where people with more power than I'd ever been close to would look at me and start talking.

Sometimes it was terrifying, but being that close to people like that felt different. Like something was possible that hadn't been before.

The rule at the desk was simple: Yahoo News was permitted. Everything else was not.

So I read Yahoo News. I'd click the same headlines more than once. Not because they'd changed. Because the act of clicking broke the silence between conversations.

I carried that into corporate. At my recruiting desk, LinkedIn was the job. Sourcing candidates. But after lunch—on the shuttle since 6 a.m., already exhausted before the day had formally begun, still facing rush hour on the peninsula and a stack of afternoon meetings—I wasn't sourcing anyone. I was scrolling. Reading posts. Watching what people were saying. Using a professional platform the way everyone uses a social one. Just with better lighting and fewer selfies.

Every day, a building full of upwardly mobile people passed my desk. Nobody saw what was forming there. I didn't either.

It didn't feel like a habit, scrolling LinkedIn. It felt like a natural way to fill the time. I didn't know I was practicing anything, of course, or conditioning myself. I just didn't want to sit there with nothing to do.

By the time I had thirty-three tabs open on my laptop, I thought it was a focus problem. I didn't know it was a practice I'd been perfecting since I was twenty-two.

The first time I pushed back, it felt like breaking a rule. I told my team I was going off the grid for a week. No Wi-Fi; you won't be able to reach me. I felt a mix of guilt and unbridled excitement, like a caged animal let free to graze.

And when I got there—lying on a black inner tube in a lazy river, staring up at the sky, surrounded by family and friends in the Redwoods—I realized how quiet my body had become. How still. How *mine* again.

If my time at Google taught me anything, it's that companies know tech is distracting. Even with offices tricked out with video conferencing in every room and bespoke platforms built for in-house use, digital boundaries were still present. We'd have what were called "laptop down" meetings, where we weren't allowed to have our computers open. Often, it was one person presenting or taking notes while the rest of the group was relegated to handwritten notes.

Phones were kept screens down. One buzz and suddenly everyone's attention shifted.

It's easy to underestimate the cost of these interruptions. In a landmark study, researcher Gloria Mark found that after an interruption, it took an average of 23 minutes and 15 seconds for workers to return to their original task. Not because they immediately stopped working, but because they often bounced through several other tasks before finding their way back.

The challenge is that interruptions aren't rare. One survey found Americans checked their phones hundreds of times per day. Even if each glance only lasts a few seconds, those moments add up, creating a state of continuous partial attention that makes sustained focus increasingly difficult.

I'm sure you've felt this, to some degree, how one minor intrusion can shatter everyone's focus. It's not just in meetings, of course. It's at dinner with friends, in conversations with your mom, and during family time. The constant ping-pull of notifications is the soundtrack of our lives. We're losing more focus time than hours we're even awake. Our brains are fragmented. No wonder we feel off, guilty that we can't keep up in a world that celebrates hustle over harmony.

Even Google's former design ethicist, Tristan Harris, admitted to struggling with distractions. Hearing him speak, I remember feeling a sense of relief that I was in good company, followed quickly by alarm that even people deeply entrenched in the industry struggle to protect their attention from the very technology they created. How did I even stand a chance when a tech titan like Tristan could barely manage?

In 1971, economist Herbert Simon warned that "a wealth of information creates a poverty of attention." When I first read that line, I felt defensive. *Poverty* felt dramatic. Then I looked at my phone: twenty-three tabs open, ten apps running in the background, eighty-six unread emails. I wasn't managing my attention—I was triaging it. Simon wasn't predicting. He was diagnosing.

Jack Dorsey built the system that proved Simon right. Twitter wasn't designed to fragment attention—but the infinite feed, the notifications, the retweets, all exploited the exact scarcity Simon identified decades earlier.

It's what I call "open-tab mind."

I tried to fix it with willpower. Deleted Instagram (came back to binge yet again). Phone in another room at night (lasted two weeks). Grayscale mode (turned off after three days because I couldn't tell which app was which). None of it stuck.

I was treating symptoms, not the actual problem.

This is the part we rarely name. The problem isn't screen time. It's unconscious time. Time spent reacting instead of choosing. Time that looks productive on the outside but feels scattered on the inside. I wasn't distracted—I was living in a constant state of response. And the longer I stayed there, the harder it became to tell where I should direct my attention in the first place.

I'm not going to do what Jack Dorsey does—ten-day silent retreats and no phone before noon. I'm not aiming for monkhood. I'm aiming for agency. And that starts with admitting something uncomfortable.

My attention had been trained without my consent.

FOCUS FARMING

The first time I truly understood what it meant to be present, I was standing on a dock in the San Juan Islands off the coast of Washington state, watching fog roll in over the water, slowly blanketing the starry sky. It was 2006. No smartphones. No feeds. Just the sound of the tide and the kind of quiet that makes you feel small in the best possible way.

Camp Nor'wester was a place where the world seemed to stand still. As a counselor, I watched kids arrive clutching their last moments of connectivity, and leave weeks later having forgotten they ever needed it. Singing and skits replaced stress. Connection flowed freely, because everyone was fully there. I could feel it then, the value of truly being able to disconnect was palpable. I didn't have a word for it yet. I just knew it felt like something I wanted to hold onto.

I held onto it as long as I could.

Then I got my first corporate job.

Visa wasn't just a job. It was *proof.* I was a first-generation college student, and landing a role at one of the most recognizable companies in the world felt like the culmination of everything I had worked toward. Finally, things were clicking. My parents were proud. I was proud. For the first time in my life, I had financial freedom, a badge that opened doors, and a seat at a table I had once only read about. It was hard, but it was fantastic. A fantasy, honestly, for someone like me.

I was a year in, still on contract, still proving myself, when everything shifted on a dark, rainy morning at the Lucky Drive bus pad. Standing in the rain, not feeling very lucky.

A dark figure appeared out of the corner of my eye. As I turned to look, I was met with a quick smile and a sigh. "I don't know where the shuttle is," she said. "There's flooding up the highway, and it might not make it."

My 2017 brain couldn't fathom the idea of not making it to the office. And from the look on her face, neither could she.

Within minutes, she had devised a plan—she would drive us the hour and a half through San Francisco into Silicon Valley herself. This wasn't just any woman. This was the vice president of HR at the company I worked for. And as the university recruiter who owned hiring for HR, I knew of her, had seen her speak, but this was another level.

I opened the door of her black Mercedes and slipped into the leather seat.

We spent the next ninety minutes talking as we fought our way down 19th Avenue. Her experiences as a recruiter before computers existed. Her retreat home in the Redwoods. But that's not what stayed with me. That's not what became the driving force that led me here.

It was a sharp comment about a blog post. One that had almost cost a candidate a coveted role because they hadn't proofread their work. It wasn't perfect. There were errors.

Lazy. Incompetent. *Next.*

And as we sat at the red light a block from the office, my world changed.

Errors were no longer an option. Errors were a weakness.

She would never know it, but that comment quietly detonated something in me. Emails took longer to write. Tasks stretched past their deadlines. Project proposals sat unsubmitted. Every Friday at Google, when packets were due, I panicked. And my blog, the one I'd been quietly building in my head for years about burnout and self-care and what it meant to live a fulfilled life, stayed blank.

Not because I didn't have something to say. Because I didn't trust myself to say it without it being perfect. Because somewhere in the back of my mind lived a voice from college that said writing was for the serious writers, the ones who could afford to choose it.

For someone like me, practicality wasn't a suggestion. It was the plan. *Who was I to think I could be a writer?* That doubtful question had always been there. The VP's comment just gave it a megaphone.

And a mind preoccupied with being perfect is a mind that can never be present.

I had stepped into the corporate fantasy and, somewhere along the way, the fantasy had started running me.

I knew something was wrong. A gap widened between the life I was building on the outside and the person I was becoming on the inside. But the only map I had back to myself was the one I'd drawn years earlier on a dock in the San Juan Islands.

So I went looking.

Camp Grounded was a full-scale adult summer camp run by Digital Detox, tucked deep in the redwood forest on the Mendocino coast. Four strangers in a car, two hours north of Marin County, heading into the trees for a weekend without technology, without names, without work talk. We laughed around the fire, had conversations that went somewhere, and sat through a silent dinner with over two hundred people. In the end, we returned to the present moment. The key takeaway: You can't download the smell of campfire.

It worked. For a weekend, I remembered what it felt like to be still.

But here's what I know now that I didn't know then: You don't need to spend hundreds of dollars and drive two hours into the woods to reclaim yourself. You can, if that's what calls you. But real reclaiming doesn't live in a weekend retreat. It lives in the small moments of everyday life: the morning you sit with your coffee before reaching for your phone, the walk you take without earbuds, the conversation during which you put the phone face down and actually listen.

The redwoods were never the point. Presence was. And presence doesn't require a reservation.

THE SILENT ALGORITHM

The most triggering post on social media for me— and for most women I know—is the engagement photo. The flawless proposal. The dream dress. The perfect life. The next morning, you're still replaying it. Doesn't matter if it's Taylor Swift and Travis Kelce's secret garden engagement seen by millions, or the friend you lost touch with years ago. The effect is the same. Then, without warning, a layoff announcement spikes your cortisol before you've even had your first cup of coffee.

Next swipe: wellness influencer with their 5 a.m. green juice as you wolf down a bagel. Linger too long, and the algorithm floods your feed with sculpted abs. What felt harmless has quietly shifted your body perception. And it doesn't stop there. One unboxing video convinces you that what was good yesterday isn't enough today. A glimpse of a stranger's villa wedding on Lake Como makes you question every life choice you've ever made up until now.

You didn't search for it, you didn't ask for it, but, even hours later, you can't stop thinking about it. Behind the scenes, the post quietly shaped your mood and self-worth. That's the danger of the silent algorithm. It steers your beliefs about yourself and the world to maximize engagement, rather than your well-being.

What feels like a coincidence is calculation—millions of micro-predictions translating your activation into amplified content. Algorithms track your scroll speed, dwell time, and hover patterns to infer your mood.

Mirror neurons mean emotional contagion spreads online through imitation and empathy loops.

And AI systems, trained on our collective behavior, are literally learning from us in real time. Your feed isn't just showing your choices. It's amplifying your emotional responses. It uses infinite scroll, autoplay, and notifications to keep you on.

Our feeds aren't optimized for truth. They don't weigh or care about value. They decide our moods and beliefs by predicting what will keep us logged on.

I'll be honest—I love the quick hits too. And even though I know better, I still struggle. Knowing that every tap, click, like, or linger is being tracked. Tracked to predict the next piece of content most likely to keep me for another minute. Delivered at the precise moment. This isn't what you asked for, but it's what will keep you. It's not just content. If it changes how you feel about yourself, it's a push.

Ask yourself: *Who benefits from me seeing this?*

MYTH OF CONTROL

I grabbed my phone to check the weather. Short sleeves or sweater? Thirty minutes later, I'd watched fifteen reels and still hadn't figured out what to wear.

I hadn't bought anything. But I knew exactly what I could have bought. A foldable at-home Pilates machine, the one that had been following me for months. I didn't plan to purchase it. The algorithm had already done the math.

It knew I'd been thinking about my arms.

It knew when to strike.

We think we're the ones doing the choosing. But we've already been chosen.

This is the myth we live inside: *I'm in charge of my feed.* The reality is quieter and far more unsettling. Your feed is in charge of you. We like to believe we're scrolling by choice, but what we experience as choice is almost always pre-framed. Algorithms decide what we see, when we see it, and how long we stay. Each "decision" arrives already shaped by predictive systems trained on our own behavior. As the line goes: You are not the user. You are the product.

I started noticing this more clearly after I began writing this book. Around the same time, several friends—who hadn't connected—each bought that exact Pilates machine. Unprompted. Within days of one another.

When they mentioned it, I wasn't surprised. I knew why. I'd been served the same ads, at the same frequency, with the same emotional timing. The difference wasn't willpower. It was awareness. I had broken the pattern just enough to see it.

The algorithm hadn't predicted their joy. It had produced it.

Within hours, they were excited, invested, reorganizing their routines around a new identity. A week later, the enthusiasm had faded.

Every scroll, click, pause, and hesitation had trained the system.

People don't discover hobbies anymore. Their feeds assign them, complete with a list of supplies, an identity, and an expiration date.

Behind the screen, thousands of data points are analyzed in real time. And it isn't just what you click. It's how long you hover. When your scrolling slows. Where your eyes linger on a face or a word. All of it is tracked, assembled into a behavioral fingerprint, and fed back to you as "personalization." The system isn't reading your mind. It's rewriting your impulses. And the more predictable you become, the easier you are to persuade.

Once, days after I'd moved somewhere new, the internet hadn't been set up yet, and I was working from home. Nothing was on fire. No one needed me urgently. But I felt it anyway—a low-grade anxiety about being offline, a guilt that felt almost physical, like I was ditching school and didn't want the teacher to find out. I kept refreshing. Kept apologizing in advance. Kept telling myself this is just how it is now. This is just what work feels like.

I didn't question it. I just accepted it as the price of being a professional in 2023.

There's a name for what I was doing in that apartment. Jean-Paul Sartre called it "bad faith."

Sartre, a twentieth-century philosopher obsessed with freedom and responsibility, argued that the most seductive form of control isn't force—it's convenience. Freedom doesn't disappear when it's constrained; it disappears when we pretend we don't have it. His most unsettling insight was simple: Not choosing is still a choice. When we tell ourselves, "This is just how things are," or, "I didn't really choose it," we're practicing bad faith, the quiet surrender of responsibility disguised as relief. We don't lose freedom because it's taken from us. We lose it because holding it requires effort, and convenience offers us an escape.

Over time, your past behavior narrows what the algorithms show you until you're living inside a feedback bubble that feels personal, but is actually predictive. The feed gets smarter, and your perspective gets smaller. Variable rewards and novelty spikes keep the dopamine flowing—not to make you satisfied, but to make you stay. The system isn't built for your fulfillment; it's built for your retention. Every ping promises meaning, only to deliver a hollow moment of distraction.

Features like Next Up and Autoplay quietly remove natural stopping points.

You don't decide to keep going; the platform decides for you. Every notification is a subtle nudge. Every scroll, a tiny surrender. Settings and toggles reinforce the illusion of control. You feel empowered adjusting preferences, even as the real levers—ranking logic, ad incentives, data monetization—remain hidden beneath the surface.

We tweak preferences while the platform tweaks us.

The cost isn't just attention. It's autonomy. The more invisible systems shape our decisions, the less we remember how to choose for ourselves. Curiosity narrows. Opinions harden. The world shrinks to fit the feed.

What's lost is quieter and harder to measure: the slow erosion of wonder. The joy of stumbling onto something unexpected without being served it. The satisfaction of deciding for yourself.

Awareness is the only real control we have left. Every time you pause before you scroll, you interrupt the loop. And that moment, when you notice the numbness, is freedom in disguise.

THE BOTTOMLESS FEED

Scrolling feels like ordering from The Cheesecake Factory's twenty-one-page menu: avocado egg rolls, Thai lettuce wraps, chopped salad, Louisiana chicken pasta, Glamburger, chicken Madeira, and every cheesecake flavor ever invented. Until we remember what we really came for: the brown bread.

It's the bottomless mimosas, the endless refills.

Yet still, somehow, we remain thirsty.

We've been sold the idea that more options mean more freedom. They don't. The feed doesn't promise happiness—it promises the possibility of it, always just one swipe away. And so curiosity quietly turns to craving as we chase the next thing, not because we need it, but because we've forgotten how to stop.

The promise of choice keeps us hooked, but choice isn't freedom when the possibilities never end. What looks like abundance is a well-designed system. We start out curious, even delighted, but somewhere between the options and overwhelm, pleasure turns to autopilot.

We stop tasting, stop noticing, stop choosing—and just keep consuming.

That's because the feed was never designed to end. Infinite scroll, autoplay, and "Recommended for You" weren't created for our benefit. They were engineered to override our natural stopping cues, the ones that tell our brains, *I'm done now.*

In 2006, designer Aza Raskin created infinite scroll, a feature that removes cues and keeps users continuously consuming content. He later called it "behavioral cocaine" and has since dedicated himself to undoing what he built—testifying against Meta for the engineering of addiction and co-founding the Center for Humane Technology to advocate for fundamental design change.

His regret isn't abstract. To protect his own focus, Raskin is rumored to work across three separate computers: one for deep work, one beside it for email and web, and a third a short walk away for Twitter and his blog. The man who engineered the endless feed built his own friction back in. That single decision to remove the bottom rewired billions of brains, including ours, to keep reaching for more.

We can spend an hour scrolling and still not remember a single thing we saw.

We believe we can stop anytime. But the truth is, we're sitting in a Waffle House at 2 a.m., bathed in fluorescent light, scrolling a menu we already know by heart. The waitress keeps topping off our coffee, the jukebox plays something we've stopped listening to, and we order another side of cheesy hash browns—not because we're hungry, but because leaving would mean admitting we've had enough.

Waffle House is famous for never closing—not for hurricanes, not for floods, not for blizzards. FEMA uses its open status as an informal disaster indicator. If a Waffle House closes, something has gone very wrong.

The feed never closes.

There's no last call. No check. No signal that you've had enough. No moment when the lights come on and someone gently suggests you head home.

Just an endless invitation to stay.

That's the secret of the bottomless feed—it doesn't end because it doesn't want you to leave. What started as connection has turned into captivity.

WHAT WE'RE REALLY REACHING FOR

For a long time, I thought my relationship with my phone was a personal failure. That I was weak. Addicted. Had bad boundaries. But the deeper I went, the more I realized something that changed everything. I wasn't reaching for my phone because I lacked discipline. I was reaching because I was trying to meet a need.

Technology didn't just give me entertainment. It gave me ease when I was overwhelmed. Distraction when I was anxious. Connection when I felt lonely. Growth when I felt stuck. Impact when I wanted to matter.

And it worked. At least, at first.

That's the trap. The system doesn't hook you by offering something you don't want. It hooks you by offering something you desperately *do*. In the last two decades, technology has quietly become the fastest way to meet five very human needs:

Ease: When life feels heavy, we want it lighter.
Distraction: When life feels too loud, we want relief.
Connection: When we feel alone, we want to be seen.
Growth: When we feel stuck, we want possibility.
Impact: When we feel small, we want to matter.

None of these needs is wrong. They're human. The problem is how we've learned to meet them. This book maps those five needs as they show up in modern life—the quiet ways we outsource them to our devices, the moments when comfort slips into autopilot, and the places where stimulation masquerades as nourishment and visibility pretends to be meaningful.

This is not so you can judge yourself.

This is so you can finally understand what's been shaping you.

CONSUMING VS. NOURISHING

I arrived at Arizona State as a seventeen-year-old freshman. I moved into Manzanita Hall, a fifteen-story dorm fueled by chaos and hormones, just steps from Sun Devil Stadium and Frat Row.

Downstairs was the all-you-care-to-eat dining hall, a place advertised to combat the Freshman Fifteen, yet engineered to make it somehow inevitable.

One swipe of my student ID and suddenly I was no longer the kid eating whatever my mom put on the table. I was living "Cheeseburger in Paradise" in real life—complete with a soft-serve machine and a waffle station that felt like a religious experience. Endless chicken nuggets and more sauces than Chick-fil-A. It was the first time in my life that "whatever your heart desires" wasn't a motivational metaphor. It was my dinner plan, and my introduction to consuming on autopilot.

That dining hall was a lesson in overfill, how too much of anything dulls the flavor. The first few days were spent in electric freedom. Two weeks later, it was routine. A month in, I could walk the entire buffet with my eyes closed. I stopped deciding and just grabbed whatever was in reach.

It took me years to realize we do the same thing online. We scroll, watch, and listen. Consuming not because we love it, or because we chose it, but because it's there.

We live in a world where digital consumption is the default, and nourishment requires intention. Screens serve endless options, causing our brains to slip into buffet mode. And much as that dining hall did decades ago, it feels like freedom, even as it becomes a trap.

Let's be clear: Consumption itself is not inherently bad. It's when we persistently, *unconsciously* consume that it becomes a problem. We are not meant to live in a state of constant intake. Our minds need pauses, our bodies need quiet, and our hearts need space to breathe.

Tech creates the opposite environment, as the pace never slows and the feed never empties. Curiosity turns into craving, output turns into overwhelm, and digital comfort turns into digital autopilot.

This world keeps handing us stimulation and calling it nourishment. It gives us distraction and calls it self-care. And we buy it not because it works, but because it's right there, waiting for us at every quiet moment. We call it relaxing, even when we log off feeling emptier than when we started.

Most of us don't even realize we've slipped into digital buffet mode. We move from app to app the way I used to move from station to station in that dining hall, grabbing whatever was closest instead of choosing what would make me feel good. Not because we're weak or undisciplined, but because the entire system is built to keep us grazing.

That's the part no one talks about.

Tech has become our default entertainer, therapist, and companion. It fills every micro-moment before we even feel it—boredom, loneliness, uncertainty, stress. We reach for the nearest screen the way a younger version of me went for the soft-serve machine. It's quick relief, fast pleasure, instant quiet, but it's not nourishment. Nourishment requires intention—noticing what something does to you, not just what it does for you.

Because digital freedom isn't about willpower.

It’s about awareness.

And we rarely stop long enough to ask the only question that matters:

Is this feeding me—or numbing me?

THE ILLUSION OF CHOICE

Free delivery, shop this week's sales, buy again, deals based on your past purchases. The Whole Foods Market app opens like a digital carnival, red and yellow discount badges flashing across every item—40 percent off with Prime, 34 percent off with Prime, 33 percent off with Prime. One tap on the yellow plus button and the item slides into your cart without hesitation, without weight, without the slight pause where your brain used to check in and ask if this is really what you wanted.

You spend an hour "shopping," although shopping doesn't feel like the right word anymore. It feels more like wandering through a maze designed from your own data, curated aisles built from previous clicks and cravings.

When you finally check out, the app interrupts you one more time: *Did you forget?*

These reminders are not random—they are calculated from years of data the system has been collecting on you. Every decline, every acceptance, every small concession becomes another prediction about what you will buy next.

On the surface, it feels like unlimited choice. In reality, it is a carefully orchestrated sequence meant to guide you toward the products that keep you in the loop the longest. So you keep spending. Behind it all is a quiet, invisible engine called *machine learning*. Where your past becomes the system's prediction of your future, and pattern recognition becomes persuasion.

I know this world because I hired the people who helped build it.

At Uber, I recruited machine-learning engineers for the Uber Eats Groceries Recommendation team, the people creating the logic that decides what shows up first and what is framed as a "deal you might like." At first, it felt helpful. Thoughtful, even. But then I started to notice that the app was not just learning from me, but quietly teaching me what to want. A gentle nudge here, a strategically highlighted discount there, all guiding my eye long before I even thought to choose.

The moment I noticed, I could never unsee it.

When we stop mistaking suggestion for desire, the system loses its grip.

I've worked for some of the most influential convenience creators in the world: Visa, Google, and Uber. Titans of ease, built on the promise that life should require as little effort as possible. Tap to pay. Ask and receive. Push a button, and anything you desire arrives like magic as we move from point A to point B, without looking out the window to notice the world passing by.

THE CONVENIENCE TRAP

It was a cold March day in Austin as music filled the small stone house that had been converted into the hip East Side bar, Whisler's. The wind had picked up, and the briskness was bone-chilling. I was freezing without a jacket, but it was too late.

I had already taken an Uber across town during the event South by Southwest (SXSW), which is one part tech conference, two parts music festival, and a whole lot of chaos. Think tech bros and electric banjos, mixed with brisket tacos and a side of queso.

It's madness. I wasn't even sure if I could get home if I wanted to. Then I remembered: I could have a hoodie delivered so I could enjoy the festival hours longer than I could have without it! It was 2016, and apps like DoorDash and Uber Eats were only two years old. The popular local app was called Favor, and it was my first experience with delivery.

With twenty bucks and a silent prayer that I wasn't being scammed, I placed my order. Meanwhile, SXSW raged all around me. If you've never been, picture this: Every bar and restaurant—or, heck, even an old house—is turned into an adult playground. Each is perfectly themed to match the company, film, or other venture sponsoring the soirée. Stages, lights, and floor-to-ceiling installations transform the ordinary world into a tech fever dream.

It's interactive and brings the whole city to life, which causes apocalyptic-level traffic jams and wait times everywhere you turn. But the chaotic genius is so contagious that one can't help but join in, even if you didn't spend a dime on a pass like me.

Then, like magic, a person appeared and handed me a black American Apparel zip-up. Saving the day, allowing me to stay.

It was my first taste of modern magic: effort outsourced, need met, dopamine delivered. I've told that story for years. I think it's one of the primary reasons I became such a delivery devotee. It also saved my life more times than I can count as a single person. No longer did I have to pull myself out of bed to get soup or medicine; it could all be delivered.

What started as an SXSW fashion emergency evolved into a sick-care delivery service via Instacart. Years later, during the Yellow Jacket protests in Paris, I was able to order a burrito and a beer without leaving my flat.

It didn't feel like giving up control. It felt like evolution. But each tap, each tracked delivery, each *Your order's on the way* notification fed something deeper than hunger. It fed my brain's bottomless craving for effortlessness.

The system was teaching me: *Why move when I can swipe?*

At first, the pull of delivery didn't feel too extreme. This changed, of course, with the arrival of COVID. When leaving your house became a matter of life and death, and all you had to look forward to was delivery. This conditioned us to see all the positives while ignoring the darker truth of what it was—and is—doing to human behavior.

I used to love grocery shopping. I looked forward to it. Fast forward six years, and I can't tell you the last time I did a full in-person shop. Somewhere along the way, the personal became universal. My habits weren't mine alone; they were the blueprint for an entire generation's new normal as we've outsourced not just our errands, but our instincts. The most minor discomforts, like hunger, boredom, and loneliness, now trigger a search bar instead of self-reflection.

We don't go to the store. Now we scroll while strangers shop for us.

We don't talk to strangers. Now we track them.

How often do you watch the tracking data to see if the driver moved four or five blocks? The more I watched, the more I realized I wasn't tracking the driver. I was tracking my own detachment.

What began as convenience became comfort. And comfort, over time, became dependence.

We didn't mean to stop showing up for life. We just started letting apps do it for us.

THE PRODUCTIVITY ILLUSION

I watched this happen on my former team. A senior manager was presenting a campus recruiting strategy to leadership—clean slides, confident delivery, the kind of meeting where you're supposed to sound decisive.

She'd used AI to help draft her notes. Nothing elaborate. Just a quick assist to streamline the talking points. Mid-presentation, she made a claim that didn't match our data—or logic, even. It sounded polished, authoritative, and wrong. The VP interrupted. "Can you explain where that insight came from?" She paused. We could see her mentally searching for it.

The truth was brutal: It was an AI hallucination. A confident sentence that had slipped through because it sounded right. She tried to recover. Smiled. Clarified. But the moment had already landed. Not because she'd used AI. But because she'd trusted it without verifying. After the meeting, no one said much. But we all knew the same thing: Writing the notes herself would've been faster. And safer.

That's what the productivity illusion sells us, that the faster path is always the better one. That offloading thinking is the same as freeing up thinking. It isn't.

We've built entire careers around the belief that being constantly connected means being consistently accomplished. That more input leads to better output. But the real cost doesn't show up in the meeting. It shows up in the pattern, the slow erosion of trusting your own thinking over the tool's.

More motion. Less meaning. A mind constantly lit up, but rarely alive.

Real productivity isn't about staying on. It's about knowing what deserves your attention and protecting it long enough to actually do something with it.

The tool isn't the problem. Outsourcing your judgment to it is.

INVISIBLE IMPACT

I've always been shy about posting, even when it comes to big wins. I remember standing at the podium at a national conference, looking out on a room full of people who had registered specifically to hear what I had to say. I had spent weeks preparing, refining, second-guessing. And when it went well, when people came up afterward and said it resonated, I felt something genuine. But the moment someone suggested I post about it, that feeling got complicated.

We measure our worth in proof, not presence.

And when proof becomes the point, even our joy starts to feel like content.

The same thing happened with my development programs. I spent years dreaming about designing programs I wish existed when I was figuring things out as a young professional. Then I built them. Led them. I watched people move through them and come out the other side with opportunities they hadn't had before.

Those moments—speaking at national conferences, hosting the president of the University of Waterloo at Uber's headquarters, attending a talk at USC with the CEO and chairman of the board as the only recruiter selected to be there—those moments should've felt like proof I'd made it. Instead, I hesitated. The captions never sounded right.

Deep down, I knew posting would be performative.

Yet not posting felt like a failure, a missed opportunity.

Success didn't feel like success unless it was seen. And that terrified me. The pressure wasn't just internal. It's systemic. We've built a culture where worth is measured in visibility, not vitality, and the moment we stop performing, we risk disappearing.

Even rest has become performative. I can still picture myself in my clawfoot bathtub, rain falling on the creek outside, a wellness podcast playing—convinced I was resting, when really I was just curating a quieter version of the grind.

We don't just work; we curate our work. We document the grind for validation, mistaking applause for alignment. Success has become something we must prove in public to believe in private. But what happens when the applause fades? Or when the algorithm changes again?

We confuse visibility with value and forget what we wanted in the first place.

But success isn't something you achieve. It's something you align with. It's the quiet confidence that comes from living your values when no one's watching.

When you stop chasing and start choosing, that's when you begin to reclaim your definition of *enough*.

Power isn't in what we turn on. It's in what we turn off.

THE VALIDATION TRAP

Some online moments feel tiny from the outside, but seismic on the inside. I'll never forget the day motivational speaker Marie Forleo shared one of my pins on Pinterest. I froze. Then squealed. Then I took a screenshot and sent it to my mom, as if it were a trophy.

The pin was simple, a guide I'd written called "How to Stop Scrolling and Start Living." It was something I believed in enough to put out into the world, not knowing if anyone would ever find it. I was still early in the process of figuring out what I was building, still in that tender stage where you're creating because it matters to you and quietly hoping it matters to someone else too.

She shared it through Tailwind, in a personal growth community—not a direct message, not a public shoutout, just a quiet re-share in a corner of the internet unnoticed by most people. But I noticed. Immediately. Because when you're still not sure if what you're making matters, even the smallest signal from the right person can feel like a lifeline.

Marie was one of those people I had studied from a distance. Someone who had built an entire world around helping people do meaningful work. When she shared it, it wasn't just a notification. It felt like confirmation. Like someone who had already walked the path I was trying to find had visited to say: *You're going the right way.*

It was a blip in her universe, a single share, but to me it felt cosmic. Validation from the Universe. That's the thing about social media—sometimes a stranger becomes a mentor, and sometimes a mentor becomes the person who hands you the courage to take the next step. But there's a quieter truth underneath moments like that, a truth most of us don't want to acknowledge.

We've built emotional ecosystems around the validation of people who don't know us.

We don't just want to be seen. We want to be *approved*.

We want confirmation that our path is right, that our work matters, that we're not falling behind. And when someone we admire validates us—even in the smallest way—it feels like evidence that everything we're doing isn't a delusion.

I've lived inside that trap. There were days when a quiet post made me question everything, and a single "like" from the right person lifted me higher than I could lift myself. What I didn't realize was that I was outsourcing my self-worth, one notification at a time.

I remember posting something I cared about, then immediately trying to act like I didn't. I closed the app, put my phone down, and told myself it didn't matter. Then I checked it anyway. Then again, and again. It was quiet. A couple of likes, but no real response. Nothing that felt like it meant anything. I felt the shift almost immediately. Not big, not dramatic. Just enough to start thinking maybe it wasn't that good, maybe I said too much, or maybe I shouldn't have posted it at all.

Nothing about the post changed. But the way I felt about it did. Suddenly I wasn't thinking about what I shared. I was thinking about whether I was someone worth listening to.

I didn't need feedback. I needed proof, and I was looking for it in the wrong place.

What makes this trap so powerful is how subtle it is. I didn't notice the shift at first: the way I started checking who viewed my stories or how I refreshed my notifications needlessly. Crafting captions that sounded more like what would perform than what I wanted to say.

Slowly, creativity becomes contingent on applause. Joy becomes conditional. And intuition becomes tangled with metrics that were never designed to measure meaning.

Validation is intoxicating because it answers the question we're all quietly asking: *Does any of this matter? Does my voice register in a world that never stops talking?* But when your value becomes tied to other people's reactions, you start living a life that isn't entirely yours. You start dimming, editing, shrinking—not for truth, but for approval.

That's the dangerous beauty of the validation trap. When the internet claps, we believe we're enough. When it's quiet, we question everything.

Then there's the flip side, the quote that cracked something open in me: "I'm not in competition with people I don't feel inspired by."

Paige DeSorbo said this on the *Giggly Squad* podcast, and cohost Hannah Berner stopped mid-conversation, like someone had just knocked the wind out of her. I dropped my head back and laughed. It was so blunt, so unapologetic, and somehow more freeing than any piece of advice I'd heard in a long time. Maybe ever.

But it didn't just make me laugh and move on. It stayed. It's still here. Because when you're building something bigger than most people around you can even imagine, there's this quiet exhaustion that comes with it—the lament of, "Why don't they *get* it?" and the endless comparisons to people who aren't even playing the same game.

Energy spent trying to justify a vision that doesn't need justifying.

That one quote cut through all of it. *I'm not in competition with people I don't feel inspired by.* Point blank.

No judgment. No explanation required. Just permission to stop measuring yourself against the wrong rulers entirely. The more I sat with it, the more I realized the women I love, admire, and study already live by that rule. They don't chase validation from rooms they don't want to be in. They don't compare themselves to people who drain them. They don't shape-shift to fit into someone else's idea of success.

They rise because they're rooted. They stay in their purpose.

Hearing Paige say it unapologetically didn't just land; it realigned something in me. It was the first time I understood that comparison and validation come from the same wound, the belief that our worth needs permission.

Once you see that, you realize the trap was never about the likes, but about forgetting that your worth was yours to name all along. And when that clicks, you see the trap for what it really is—not a game you're losing, but a game you never needed to play.

THE MYTH OF "CONNECTION"

The waves crashed violently on the sandy shore as a lifeguard scanned the waterline, whistle poised at his lips. It was red-flag day on Medano Beach, one of the few swimmable stretches in Los Cabos. The wind whipped the flags into a frenzy, their crimson fabric snapping like warning shots against the cloudless sky. Beyond the roped-off safe zone, the Pacific churned, dark and restless, frothing white where it collided with volcanic rock.

Inside the resort, insulated from the ocean's rage by thick glass and carefully landscaped palms, the lobby bar hummed with the manufactured ambiance of vacation: clinking ice cubes, soft jazz, the occasional burst of laughter from couples who'd already had one too many by noon.

Sean and I met Ben at the lobby bar. He was waiting for his friend, swirling an amber drink in a crystal tumbler. If you've ever been to Cabo, you know there are two types of people: those who are looking for connection, and those who would rather not be bothered. Within a few seconds of eye contact, you can usually figure out which one a person is.

Ben was looking for connection. And as a shy late bloomer who had just started my first business—a wellness brand I was building from scratch on social media—I suddenly had plenty to say after two mezcalitas. The smoky liquor had loosened something in my chest, untying the knot of self-doubt I always carried with me.

He asked about my plans to become an influencer. His tone was flat, almost clinical. I corrected him—a *wellness* influencer, I explained, smiling. There was a difference. I was trying to help people find balance. Mind-body connection, stress management, that kind of thing. I pulled out my phone without thinking, opening Instagram to show him my carefully curated feed. Daily self-care tips, ritual guides, motivational quotes.

His voice cut through the bar noise like a blade: "Put that away."

I froze, my thumb hovering over the screen.

"Put it away," he repeated.

His eyes, which had seemed pleasant enough moments ago, had hardened into something else entirely. The warmth of the mezcal turned cold in my veins. What I had thought was a lighthearted conversation about my dreams was turning into something else entirely—his telling me all the reasons that it was a bad idea.

I wasn't helping people. I was feeding the machine. I was part of the problem.

He leaned forward, his knuckles white around his glass. Every post, every story, every notification—it was all designed to hook people. To keep them scrolling. To make them feel like they were never enough without whatever was being sold.

At first, I was offended. My face flushed hot, and I felt that familiar defensive anger rising in my throat. Who was this man to attack my dreams? To judge something he knew nothing about? I'd worked so hard to build my confidence, to finally put myself out there after years of playing small, and here was some random stranger at a hotel bar tearing it all down.

But I've been around long enough to know that when someone has a reaction this visceral—especially to a stranger—it's not personal. There's always something underneath, something bigger pressing on them from the inside.

So I listened, took a slow breath, and reached for my water glass instead of my phone.

"Tell me what happened," I said.

Not as a question. Just permission.

It took time—minutes that felt like hours—but once his anger subsided, I saw it. A deep sadness haunted his eyes. It had been there all along, just hidden behind the rage. As I stared back at him with concern, genuinely worried now about this man I'd just met, he softened. His shoulders dropped. He set down his glass with a trembling hand. His voice came slowly, with almost no emotion, as if he'd told this story so many times that the words had worn smooth. He'd lost his wife and daughter to TikTok addictions. The bar noise seemed to recede. I heard my own heartbeat in my ears.

"What do you mean, 'lost'?" I asked quietly.

He looked up. "They're alive," he said. "But they're gone."

He stared back at his hands. All they did was watch videos. Just videos. All day, all night. He'd tried to talk to them. Begged them to just look up, to see what was happening. But it was like they couldn't hear him anymore. He talked about the fights. The therapy sessions that didn't work. And the moment he realized his wife was choosing the screen over their marriage.

I felt my throat tighten. I told him I was sorry. But was I? Because I was about to do the same thing to other people's families.

I interrupted, but my voice wavered. "I'm not like that," I said, maybe a little too quickly. "I'm using it for good. Wellness content, mindfulness—I want to help people." He looked at me with a bit of heard-it-before scorn, but I kept going anyway. "This is a means to an end for me. I'm in control."

Even as I said it, I could hear how it sounded. I felt the hollowness of my words. I thought about that morning, how I'd checked my phone before I even got out of bed. How I'd refreshed my notifications during the ride to the airport, in the security line, and on the plane. How my first thought upon arriving at this beautiful resort had been about the lighting for photos, not the actual ocean in front of me.

He asked if I was really in control. I wanted to argue, to tell him about my mission, my purpose, how I was different from all the other influencers out there. But the truth was sitting heavily in my chest, impossible to ignore.

Deep down, it was killing me.

We sat in silence for a long moment. Through the windows, I could see a family sitting in the lobby—mother, father, two kids. All four of them staring at their phones.

After the suitcases were emptied and the leaves turned color, the holidays were upon us. November bled into December in a blur of pumpkin-spice everything and *prematurely* premature Christmas music. The days grew shorter. My screen time grew longer.

I had almost forgotten about my near epiphany in Mexico, choosing instead to relegate the memory to that mental drawer where we stuff the uncomfortable truths we're not ready to confront. Ben's face would surface sometimes when I was scrolling late at night, his sad eyes reflected in my phone's glow, but I'd push the thought away and keep swiping.

I went on with my life, thinking this feeling was normal, that this was just life in 2023. Everyone felt this constant low-grade anxiety, right? This compulsion to check, to refresh, to see what we were missing? The tension headaches and the tight feeling in my chest and the way I snapped at my partner over nothing were all just part of being an adult, being busy, being alive in the modern world.

I told myself I was building something meaningful. That the likes and follows and comments meant I was helping people. That it was worth it. But late at night, when the phone finally slipped from my tired hands and my eyes burned from the blue light, I'd remember the way Ben's voice had cracked when he said his daughter's name. And I'd wonder if I was lying to myself about all of it.

The waves were still crashing somewhere on a beach in Mexico. The red flags were still flying. But I was already drowning, and I didn't even know it yet.

As a first-generation Facebook user, I got my first cell phone at sixteen, right alongside the keys to an '85 Corolla hatchback. That Nokia phone with pink cover felt like freedom. It became a leash.

I often think about simpler times: riding bikes until dusk and the smell of jasmine on a warm summer night. The sound of laughter over a game of dominoes after a family dinner. A time when people weren't distracted by devices or mesmerized by their feeds. Which is probably why this next observation hit me the hardest. It was Christmas Eve. I remember it vividly: my seventy-year-old parents' faces lit up by their screens—heads down, scrolling for hours as we spent the holiday together. It felt like I'd lost them, a feeling only magnified by the fact that this was the very house I'd grown up in before the internet existed. We were in the same room, but I could have been 1,800 miles away.

We scroll past the people we love to connect with complete strangers. We scroll not to feel better, but to feel less. To relax and unwind, which is often code for "numbing ourselves" to the point where we can't feel a thing. It's the digital glass of wine to take the edge off, a hit you can take anytime, anywhere.

And if you lose your phone, you could lose your mind. Maybe you've felt this before. The power goes out or the connection drops. Your mind spirals, your heart races, you begin bargaining, but it's no use. We call it FOMO, or the fear of missing out, but it's not fear at all. It's withdrawal.

The problem behind the problem isn't the phone in your hand. It's the wound in your heart, the wound of feeling like you're not enough. We seek external validation to heal the hurt left by a world more interested in clout than genuine connection—confusing likes with intimacy. We're constantly connected, yet emotionally absent from our lives. We know it feels bad, but we struggle to understand how to stop, how to put down the phone and walk away.

Caged by convenience, seduced by scrolls, it's all reward and no risk—or so we think.

We've never been more connected, yet never lonelier.

The cost? The people we love.

Who did you scroll past in your real life this week?

FINDABLE

I went to Santa Cruz to see Sara, a former philosophy advisee turned close friend. It was the kind of weekend where you say yes to everything, the way you did in your twenties.

We turned off the main mountain highway at dusk, winding down a long one-lane driveway into the dark. Headlights flashed in the distance as a green Tesla pulled over to let us pass.

An extensive private property that draws the same people back year after year—fairy lights in the redwoods, a tiki-hut treehouse DJ set, a yurt village—and inside it, an old converted school bus where we found ourselves talking too much. The free kind of talking, with no filter, no calculation. We were the kind of people you become when nobody is watching too closely. There, among people who were actually present, life suddenly opened and possibilities felt endless.

Then someone pulled out their phone to find a friend. The location wasn't loading in the forest. Everyone laughed. Then I realized everyone around the circle was sharing theirs. Each one of them had a dozen dots on their map. Friends, partners, siblings—a whole network of people who knew exactly where they were at any given moment.

I had one. My mom.

When did I become the weird one?

Nobody decided to do it. That's the part that stayed with me. There was no moment where they weighed it, considered it, chose it. It was just on. Just normal. Someone always knowing where you are, and nobody finding that strange anymore. Not even here.

Even here.

The dot was on.

Not because anyone was worried. Not because anyone was in danger. Just because that's what we do now.

We watched the sunrise from the yoga deck. Dew dripped from the white yurts. Nobody checked their phone. Nobody needed to know where anyone was. We were just there, all of us, in the same place at the same time.

We used to just call this being somewhere.

Now we call it going off the grid.

HOLLOW HEARTS

On Instagram, a heart is supposed to mean something—connection, appreciation, support. But somewhere along the way, the heart became hollow. We tap twice without thinking. We like posts we barely see. We scroll past moments that look like intimacy, even though neither of us is really there.

A heart used to be a symbol of love. Now it's a unit of measurement. A score. A signal. A tiny hit of "you matter" that fades before your thumb even lifts from the screen.

I learned that the hard way during my BossBabe Influencer School days. The reel was simple—just me sitting in my car at a local car wash, laughing at the fact that it was decidedly not Disneyland, using the trending Kris Jenner audio of her losing her mind over suds and lights, with a caption about finding joy in the small moments and manifesting your dreams. It was spontaneous, a little silly, genuinely me.

Then it hit 39,000 views. The hearts came pouring in, and I watched the numbers climb in real time from the same car, in the same driveway, suddenly feeling like a very different person than the one who had posted it twenty minutes earlier. The algorithm had decided I was interesting, and strangers agreed. I should have felt validated. I should have felt *seen*.

Instead, I felt exposed. Each heart felt heavier than the one before it, like someone tapping on the surface of a life I wasn't sure I wanted people to see. I'd grown up in the country with parents who preferred privacy over dinner parties. Our lives happened behind closed doors, in quiet rooms where nobody performed anything for anyone. And suddenly here I was, standing in a spotlight I'd turned on myself, watching strangers double-tap their way into my life, my thoughts, my carefully angled vision board.

The weight wasn't just about being seen—it was about how I was being seen. Every heart felt like a vote of interest in a life I wasn't sure was interesting enough. My life felt ordinary to me. Would I have to perform extraordinariness now? Would I need to live in rooms with white walls and perfect lighting, editing my days into highlight reels, recording intimate moments for people I'd never meet?

The reel had opened a door I didn't know how to close, and on the other side was this quiet terror: What if they found out there wasn't much to see? Or, worse, what if maintaining their interest meant I'd have to stop living privately, stop being the person I'd always been, and become someone constantly available for consumption?

The hearts kept coming, and with each one, I felt the gap widen between who I was and what my account was becoming.

For the longest time, I convinced myself I avoided posting for safety, scared someone would steal my dog or find where I lived from one photo. But deep down, the truth was simpler: Being seen felt dangerous. Every time I pressed post, it felt like I was shattering into a million pieces, scattered across a feed I couldn't control.

What people don't talk about is how visibility changes the way you breathe. Even when you love creating, there is a moment right before you hit post when your whole body hesitates. Not because you doubt your worth, but because you sense the weight of all the eyes you cannot see.

There is a loneliness to posting, as well. A quiet ache that comes with sharing something meaningful and not knowing how it will land, or if it will be misunderstood, or if the wrong person will twist it into something it was never meant to be.

That quiet ache was what I carried. Not failure. Not shame. Just the tenderness of someone still learning how to be seen without disappearing inside it.

Visibility is a gift, but it's also a risk. Before I understood that, I spent years hiding from it.

When my video went viral, the idea of being "known" terrified me in a way I couldn't capture in words. So I went back to my life, convinced I was a failed influencer.

But even then, I never stopped following influencers. In fact, I loved them more. Because now I understand the courage behind every post, every reel, and every seemingly effortless moment.

People joke about brain rot and endless scrolling, but the right creator turns a guilty pleasure into a guiding light. Sometimes the content you think you're scrolling for fun is reminding you that you're not alone.

Hollow hearts are what we get from mindlessly scrolling. But the right creators can bring you back to yourself. They make the digital world feel human again. That is the power of social media when it is used intentionally—the part no one ever talks about.

THE UNPOSTED LIFE

It was a rainy November evening as I nervously opened the door to the Portal, a members-only club oozing otherworldly elegance. I slipped off my shoes and ascended the staircase to the second floor that was filled with oversized velvet couches and adorned with eclectic Eastern decor, the kind of room that makes you lower your voice automatically.

I couldn't remember how I'd found this place online, but I was eager to hear from the three authors slated to speak. Specifically, Stanford faculty member Caitlin Krause, who would be doing a reading from her new book *Digital Wellbeing*.

I didn't make eye contact with anyone, just found a cozy spot in the back corner to sit. Eager to listen but terrified to speak, I felt like an outsider as a non-member ticket holder. Yet deep down I knew I was exactly where I was meant to be. I switched off my phone and settled in for an evening of shared ideas, sans smartphones.

My heart sank as, in the front row, a man and a woman held up their phones and began recording. I think we've all been there, forced to experience life through someone else's screen. A talk with a tech CEO, a sold-out concert, or a visit to a famous landmark like the beloved Golden Gate Bridge. A recording that will either be uploaded to social media within minutes for vanity views or never be viewed again.

This was something I'd expect at a Taylor Swift concert, or Kendrick Lamar's historic show at The Forum. Certainly at the Louvre's queue for the Mona Lisa. But here at the Portal? Was nowhere sacred? It's such a prevalent problem that even bubblegum Netflix shows like *Emily in Paris* have highlighted it with lines such as, "Look with your eyes, not your phone."

To be clear, I'm not above any of this. I've felt that tug myself. The itch to capture instead of witness, to post instead of feel, to make a moment "count" by making it visible. I've caught myself rewriting captions while the world was happening in front of me.

It's a strange kind of disconnection, being physically present but mentally somewhere else.

Moments pass through our hands like water when we're too busy trying to hold them still.

We've tied our value to being seen online, forgetting the quiet power of privacy. Somewhere along the way, we began performing our lives more than participating in them. And beneath it all is the cultural myth almost everyone feels but rarely names: *"If I don't post it, it didn't happen."*

It's not our fault. We've been conditioned by social reward loops, comparison culture, and a decade-long joke—*pics, or it didn't happen*—that secretly trained us to document everything so we wouldn't disappear. But here's the real emotional truth: Every year, more strangers wish me happy birthday on LinkedIn than people who know me. It's a strange loneliness, being visible without being known.

The Portal reminded me of something essential. Some of the most sacred memories are the ones no one else sees. The ones that stay whole because they weren't interrupted, that feel alive because we didn't stop to turn them into content. They belong to us because they were lived, not captured.

Do you recognize any of these? The urge to capture instead of experience. The relief that fades faster each time. The habit of staying busy so you don't have to feel. The quiet sense that something important keeps slipping through.

If you do, nothing is wrong with you. You've been meeting real needs in the fastest way available. This chapter wasn't meant to shame you. It was meant to help you notice. Because awareness is the moment before change.

PROOF OF LIFE

The night was exactly what it was supposed to be.

Champagne. Smoke machines. Staff in motorcycle helmets riding on shoulders through the crowd, bottles raised, sparklers shooting upward toward the ceiling—spectacular, blinding, worth every penny of the table minimum.

The basement was packed, the music loud, the ceiling low. Two hundred people had come to ring in the new year in one of the most expensive ski resorts in the world, and the room was delivering. Someone raised a phone. Then another. Then everyone.

That part was also exactly what it was supposed to be.

A sparkler caught the ceiling. Slowly, at first—the kind of slowly that looks like it might still be part of the show. One young man beat at the flames on the low ceiling of the basement bar with his jacket. Around him, others danced. Some cheered. Phones stayed up—this would surely go viral. Nobody knew yet what it would become.

Within ten seconds, the entire club was on fire.

Forty-one people died.

Someone always has a phone out. At concerts, at protests, at crashes on the freeway where traffic slows not from debris, but from morbid curiosity. We have trained ourselves to reach before we react, to frame before we feel. The first instinct is no longer to move. It is to document.

We have a name for organisms that evolve toward their own extinction. Darwin called it natural selection. We just never thought we'd be the ones selected out.

The cruelest irony is not that people filmed. It is that filming had become so automatic that for some, it delayed the moment they registered what was happening. The phone went up before the body moved. They filmed because they were doing exactly what we taught them to do: Reach for your phone. Capture the moment. Prove you were there.

We spent a decade and a half conditioning an entire generation to treat intensity as content, and the burning ceiling was, by every metric the algorithm ever taught them, the most intense thing in the room.

The performance doesn't stop because something is wrong. If anything, something going wrong is more content, not less.

Then the comments came. *They should have run. Why didn't they move?* All from the same people who double-tap aspirational content, who watch disaster footage on loops, who built their own highlight reels of nights just like that one—judging, from the safety of the very platform that loaded the reflex in the first place. That is the irony that doesn't get named. We watched them do something uncomfortably familiar, and called it a failure of instinct rather than a triumph of conditioning.

We adapted. Magnificently, fatally, we adapted to the world we built—a world where the proof of living became more instinctive than the act of surviving.

The sparklers were spectacular. They always are. That's not an accident. That's the design.

—

Proof of Life is written in response to the fire at Le Constellation in Crans-Montana, Switzerland, on January 1, 2026. It is dedicated to those who died.

WITHDRAWAL

I thought unplugging would be freeing, but I was wrong.

October 4, 2021, felt like a glitch in reality. I remember exactly where I was—phone in hand, refreshing out of habit—when suddenly, nothing loaded. I checked again. Still nothing. Switched apps. Same thing. Then my group chat lit up—not on WhatsApp, but SMS. The old way. The backup plan nobody had used in years. *Is Instagram down for you? Facebook too?*

It wasn't just me. It was everyone.

For seven hours, the platforms that quietly held our conversations, plans, and daily rhythms just disappeared. Event organizers switched back to email. Students abroad were suddenly unreachable. People who hadn't sent a text in months were sending them again just to figure out where to meet for dinner.

And in that pause, something uncomfortable surfaced. Not because we missed the content. Because we realized how much of our lives only existed there—our plans, our people, our sense of what was happening in the world. We hadn't just handed over our attention. We had handed over ourselves.

It wasn't just an outage. It was withdrawal, playing out in real time, on a public—even global— stage.

Withdrawal isn't dramatic. It's familiar. It's the same way I feel when I skip my morning coffee. Or when I leave the house without my phone, even as my hand keeps reaching for it, forgetting it's not there. It's refreshing my inbox even though I know there's nothing new, or panicking when I realize I forgot to download the in-flight entertainment before a four-hour flight.

It's watching the Wi-Fi symbol cycle endlessly, feeling my whole chest tighten as if the world has frozen.

It hides in the little moments: fidgety fingers, underlying irritability, the way my mind secretly creates lists. Lists of things to remember to look up later, just to avoid surrendering to the silence. I'm haunted by phantom vibrations, pulled by the urge to check just one more time.

It's not uncommon to feel worse before feeling better. Why? My brain expects the hit. I feel irritable and restless as the cravings and discomfort throw my mind and body off balance.

Tech is built on reinforced learning loops. When we experience silence, it often registers as distress, as if we've lost oxygen, not just Wi-Fi. Yet the narrative we're sold is the opposite, as if silence is an add-on treatment at your favorite day spa. You thought it would leave you feeling rejuvenated, yet it feels more like punishment.

But it's not. It's withdrawal.

"Pleasure is the bait. Discomfort is the withdrawal." —Anna Lembke

The pain goblin arrives uninvited, but right on schedule. When you remove the stimulus, the scroll, the refresh, the constant drip of novelty, your brain doesn't just miss it. It protests. Loudly.

It manifests as physical discomfort: restlessness in your limbs, a crawling sensation under your skin, the inability to sit still. It's the feeling that something is wrong, even when nothing is. Your body has learned to associate stillness with danger, and now it's sounding every alarm it has.

This isn't metaphorical. It's neurochemical. Your brain has been flooded with dopamine for so long that the baseline feels like a deficit. The pain goblin is your nervous system's tantrum—a biochemical demand for the hit you've denied it.

This isn't weakness. It's the first sign of healing. Naming it normalizes the discomfort and reinforces that you're not broken—you're detoxing. You'll feel anxious and itchy as the cravings intensify. This discomfort is part of your nervous system recalibrating. Not proof you can't do it.

So how do you fight back? The pain goblin lies. It tells you that you need to check, that this discomfort is unbearable, that just one scroll will make it stop. And here's the trick: It will. Temporarily. That's why the loop is so hard to break.

But each time you don't feed it, the pain goblin gets a little quieter. Not immediately—it might get even louder, like a toddler escalating a tantrum. But eventually it learns. Your nervous system remembers how to regulate itself without constant stimulation.

The discomfort isn't permanent. It's a phase. And on the other side of the pain goblin's tantrum is something we've almost forgotten: the ability to be still without distress.

THE UNRAVELING

I kept arriving at the same place. Different city, different badge, different title. Same ceiling. Same crash. The first time, I didn't call it burnout. I called it a hard week and kept going.

I was under a big white tent at the UCLA Career Fair, the final stop on a two-week recruiting trip. Chicago, then Austin, now LA. My friends in Austin had pulled me aside days earlier, their voices careful, their eyes concerned. I'd laughed it off. I was fine. I was a professional. I had a nationwide primary-care membership precisely for moments like this—I could see a doctor in any city, any time. The fact that I needed this kind of coverage should have told me something. It didn't.

That morning under the tent, my volunteer looked at me and said one word: *Go.*

I took an Uber back to the W Hotel and crawled under the covers. When I woke, the sky had turned purple. I ordered room service—something I could eat in bed—and opened my laptop. I told myself I'd just catch up on a few emails. Just to stay on top of things. That's what I always did. That's what made me good at my job, an asset.

Later that evening, I made a phone call that terrified me. I called the global vice president of university recruiting and told her I couldn't travel for the rest of the season. For a recruiter, this is career suicide. I was a contractor on the conversion track, one step away from full time. I was supposed to be indispensable, tireless, always on. Instead, I was asking for help.

She was kind. She told me to take care of myself. She told me it would be okay.

I thought I'd learned something.

Two years later, I was sitting in a conference room in Mountain View, placing a red rescue inhaler on the table in front of my manager. My hands were shaking. My chest felt tight. I didn't know what was happening to me—only that I couldn't breathe the way I used to, that stairs had become a problem, that something in my body had fundamentally broken.

Stress-induced asthma, the doctor would later tell me. But at that moment, all I felt was shame.

The unraveling had been slow. It started the way it always did: staying logged on a little longer, checking Slack one more time before bed, letting the screen become the last thing I saw at night and the first thing I reached for in the morning.

It was dedication, I told myself. I was being responsible. Available. Trustworthy. I wasn't numbing—I was working. And on weekends, when the anxiety became unbearable, I'd lose myself in Netflix marathons, in food, in anything that could make me feel less.

I thought I was handling it. I thought this was what high performance looked like.

Two months later, on a crisp San Francisco morning, I was walking to One Market Plaza. I was thirty pounds heavier. I could barely climb a flight of stairs. Google had given me two "needs improvement" reviews, which, in Google speak, meant I was one misstep from being fired. But I kept showing up. I had to. If I could just work harder, perform better, prove I belonged.

Instead, I had an asthma attack behind a potted plant because I couldn't find a conference room fast enough. I couldn't ask for help. So I hid, gasping, my inhaler clutched in my hand, praying no one would see me like this. Praying I could just get through the day.

I looked at my reflection in the bathroom mirror afterward and didn't recognize the person staring back.

That was my rock bottom.

DOPAMINE DREAMS

Do you remember when Instagram Reels were released? It was August 2020, the peak of the pandemic, when screens were our only form of connection. In a mere instant, our lives changed as we became mesmerized by seven-to fifteen-second videos. It got so bad for me that Sean started making a sound to snap me out of it: "Zz-zz. Zz-zz." At first it was cute, a safe word that broke the trance and brought me back to the real world.

We've all been there. You're trying to talk to someone, but they're gone. Eyes down, thumb moving, just one more second. Or maybe it's you. Your dog is waiting. Someone's speaking. And there's a flicker of irritation, like real life is interrupting something more important.

I remember a walking meeting with an engineering manager I'd recruited for. We were moving through Sankofa Square, Toronto's version of Times Square, on our way to get food from the region of China he was from. Then he said something that stopped me mid-stride. Not because it was shocking. Because it was casual. Like he was telling me something everyone already knew.

"It's not a bug," he said. "It's by design."

That's the part most people miss. What feels like distraction is often relief. A buzz, a pause, a moment of boredom, something small, and your body moves before you've decided anything. Thumb to screen. A quick hit. A slight release. Then again. And again. We call it a dopamine loop. Call it what it is: a pattern of relief. Not FOMO. Not even choice, most of the time.

Relief.

That's why just one more never lands. The cue arrives, a buzz, a moment of boredom, a silence that asks something of you. Your body answers before your brain has made a decision. The craving isn't for content. It's for the spike. The momentary release. The tiny exhale that tells your nervous system that it can stop bracing for a second.

And it works. Every time. Just not for long enough.

So you reach again.

It was never about the content. It was the spike.

UNPLUGGED + UNCOMFORTABLE

Power outages in the digital age are problematic. But they're also telling. They illuminate the shadow side of our relationship with technology.

The lights went out at 8 p.m. No flickering, no dimming—just gone. The apartment filled with silence I didn't know could exist. No hum of the refrigerator, no whir of the router, no ambient electronic pulse. This was primeval silence. I looked out across the marina and saw nothing. No streetlights, no dock lights, just a sea of darkness that made going outside feel unsafe. I was alone.

My first move was practical, almost automatic: *I can hotspot from my phone and finish this episode.* Bridgerton, *maybe?* Emily in Paris? I can't remember now, and that's the point—it wasn't about the content. It was about my ability to escape, to not be where I was. The hotspot worked for a few minutes, then gave up. *Fine. It'll only be an hour or two.*

I reloaded the PG&E outage page. Then again. As if persistence alone might restore the grid.

An hour became two. The panic started as a whisper: *How long is this going to be?* I felt disconnected. Not from people, but from myself, from my sense of productivity, from my ability to function. *What if something were to happen?* The question was vague but urgent. *What if there were an emergency? What if—*

Is this really how people used to live? Up with the sun, down with the sun?

I looked around my apartment and realized everything required the one resource I didn't have. No control. I was spinning downward, clinging to my phone like a life raft, watching the battery percentage drop. Twenty percent. Fifteen. Ten.

I had to sit where I was. I had to be present. It wasn't a choice; it was reality staring me back in the face.

When my phone finally died, I lay in bed and tried to sleep. But my mind wouldn't stop. Would the power be back in the morning? Would I be able to make coffee? Take the Zoom call? What about the groceries I'd just bought? Would they spoil?

At 2 a.m., I got up and flipped the light switch. Nothing. Back to bed.

At 4 a.m., I heard it: the microwave beeping its stupid little victory song. Then the flashing lights as my printer reconnected to the Wi-Fi, desperate and eager, as if it too had been anxiously waiting for the power to come back on.

Relief washed over me. Not because I needed anything. I was still in bed, still trying to sleep, but I knew I had power again. That ambient hum of infrastructure, of possibility, of escape. I fell asleep almost immediately, content in knowing I had power.

But I still think about those beeps at 4 a.m. The microwave and the printer lurching back to life in the dark. And me, lying there in bed, finally able to rest. Not because I was safe, but because I was connected again.

Unplugging isn't glamorous. It's uncomfortable. And when the power finally comes back on, most of us don't sit with what we learned in the dark. We just reach for our phones and disappear again.

DIGITAL GRIEF

The ache that rose in the silence wasn't boredom. It was mourning. I was mourning the quiet loss of time, identity, and presence, an invisible ache that lived in the spaces I had filled with noise. The warmth of presence traded for the cold glow of a screen.

When notifications stop, the silence can feel scary. We misread calm as loss, and withdrawal as failure, as though stillness means we're being left behind. But the ache that surfaces when you unplug isn't emptiness—it's everything you've ignored returning for you.

I watched this play out as a camp counselor. On the first day, many of the ten-year-old boys arrived clutching their handhelds like life vests. Before the devices were collected at check-in, they were already deep in debrief, trading stories about their characters, mourning the weeks of no gameplay ahead of them. They couldn't understand how they were expected to survive without their devices. The constant refrain those first few days was some version of *if I only had my games, if I only had my controller, if I only had one hour.*

By day three, something shifted. Not dramatically, just quietly, the way light changes in the late afternoon. They stopped talking about what they didn't have and started noticing what was there. The water. The trees. The kid in the next bunk who turned out to be genuinely funny.

By the end of those weeks, they had canoed around the island, slept under stars on overnight trips, and spent a whole summer living seaside in teepees. Land stewardship and sunshine. Fresh coastal air and conversations that went somewhere because there was nowhere else to be. They had been bored, really bored, and survived it. More than survived it.

It only took a few days for them to remember how to look up and laugh. How to be bored without reaching for something to fill it. How to breathe deeply without the weight of manufactured missions and constant competition. The technology hadn't gone anywhere. But for a few weeks, neither had they.

Digital grief is the quiet mourning for what technology has cost us. It's the empty feeling after you've spent an hour scrolling and can't remember a single thing you saw. It's realizing the version of you online speaks louder than the one sitting here, quiet and unsure what to say without an audience.

That's the paradox of digital grief: You have to feel the loss before you can feel alive again.

Who are you when the scroll stops?

WHAT YOU TRADED

What moment of presence did you trade for your last scroll?

I'll go first: Waking up and reaching for my phone before my feet hit the floor. Not because the world needed me, but because I needed something to stuff the silence before it could say anything. On my commute, looking down instead of out the window, arriving somewhere before I even looked up. On the couch with my dog, him right there waiting for me, and choosing my phone instead. At dinner, scrolling news between bites, barely tasting the food, barely registering I was even there. Lying in bed at night, already exhausted, telling myself just a quick check and then losing the last few minutes of the day without noticing.

None of these moments was big. That's the point.

They were small, quiet, easy to replace, and that's exactly how they disappeared.

But the reaching wasn't random.

Underneath it is something most of us don't say out loud: that we don't know who has our information anymore. That we've handed our whole lives to systems we don't control. That AI is coming for the one thing we're good at. That our kids are growing up in something we don't understand, and we're supposed to somehow guide them through it.

That everyone else figured this out before we did, and we're already behind. That we don't trust ourselves online—or who we're becoming because of it. That the more we share, the less anything feels like ours. That we're going to say something wrong, and it's going to follow us. That if people saw the real us, they wouldn't like us.

And the quietest one of all: that we're going to put ourselves out there, and no one's going to care.

Most people don't realize how much of their digital life is built around avoiding one of these. Not fixing it. Not solving it.

Avoiding it.

Some of these fears are real. Some of them you inherited—from headlines, from peers or family members, from stories, from watching what happened to other people. But if you don't name them they quietly start making decisions for you.

DISCOMFORT BY DESIGN

If silence feels uncomfortable, it's because your brain sees stimulation as safety.

And that's not accidental. It's intentional design. Platforms capitalize on moments of unease—red dots, sound cues, scarcity language, social streaks, and the simple fact that a *Read* receipt can transform calm into chaos almost instantaneously.

That's the profit model: Discomfort is currency.

Every pang of boredom is someone else's profit opportunity.

If the system erases agency, healing begins by rebuilding it. But before you can rebuild, you have to see what you're working with. Not the polished version. The real one. I started tracking my mood around my phone use, using only a physical notebook and honest time stamps.

What I found wasn't dramatic. It was worse than dramatic.

It was ordinary.

6:12 a.m. Checked my phone before my feet touched the ground. Told myself it was just to check the time. Looked up and it had been thirty-five minutes. Can't remember the specifics of what I watched. Already feel a little behind.

10:37 a.m. Have a deadline coming up. Haven't started. Opened Instagram instead. Told myself it was just a quick break. Doesn't feel like a break. Feels like avoiding.

12:00 p.m. Lunchtime! Opened my phone before the first bite. Told myself I'd just check one thing while I ate. Finished the whole plate without tasting it.

3:10 p.m. Sat with Ziggy for a bit. He waited patiently, staring at me while I stayed on my phone instead of giving him attention. Felt weirdly aware of it but still didn't stop.

6:22 p.m. Checked my screen time. Didn't like it. Put my phone face down like that was going to fix something. Picked it up again not long after.

8:04 p.m. Sean made that sound again. "Zz-zz. Zz-zz." I looked up for a second and laughed. Picked up my phone again for no real reason, and kept scrolling.

Nothing about that day was unusual. That's what made it hard to look at. The first thing I changed wasn't dramatic either. I muted notifications—news, promotions, algorithmic nudges, anything that wasn't a real person trying to reach me. Not forever. Just long enough to notice what my nervous system did when the pings stopped.

What I noticed was the itch. The reach. The phantom pull toward a phone that wasn't buzzing.

That's when I understood that the problem wasn't the notifications, but what I had trained myself to expect from them. That's where friction begins—as information. The discomfort you feel when the pings stop isn't a sign something is wrong. It's the first honest signal you've had all day.

Friction has been mischaracterized as a problem to solve. We've been taught that ease equals progress, that smoothness is success, and that anything requiring effort must be inefficient or broken. But in a world optimized to remove resistance, friction has quietly become one of the last remaining signals of choice.

When technology works exactly as designed, it removes every pause. No loading screens. No endings. No moments to ask,

Do I want to keep going? Frictionless systems don't just save time; they bypass reflection. And without reflection, there's no agency—only momentum.

That's why friction feels so uncomfortable now. Not because it's harmful, but because it's unfamiliar. A pause feels like something is missing. Silence feels like something is wrong. Stillness feels like a void that needs to be filled.

But what's happening in those moments isn't failure—it's reorientation. It's your nervous system recalibrating after years of being trained to equate stimulation with safety.

Friction is the moment when the system releases its grip. When you mute notifications and feel restless, that's not proof you made a mistake. When you close an app and feel an urge to reopen it seconds later, that's not a lack of discipline. When boredom, irritation, or unease rises, it isn't a sign that technology was helping you cope—it's evidence that it was buffering you from yourself.

And that buffering comes at a cost. Constant stimulation trains the brain to outsource regulation. Instead of learning how to sit with uncertainty, boredom, or discomfort, we learn how to escape it. Over time, the ability to tolerate stillness weakens, and friction begins to feel threatening rather than informative.

But friction is where choice lives. It's the space between impulse and action. The beat before you click. The breath before you respond. The moment when you remember that you don't have to do what the system expects next.

This is why rebuilding friction is one of the most radical acts of digital well-being. Not dramatic disconnection. Not quitting modern life. But intentionally reintroducing small amounts of resistance—enough to slow the loop, enough to make your participation conscious again.

When you add a timer to an app, you're not limiting yourself; you're restoring an ending. When you wait ninety seconds before checking, you're not denying relief; you're giving your nervous system a chance to settle on its own. When you choose to do something the slower way—writing by hand, shopping in person, listening to music without skipping—you're practicing presence, not nostalgia.

Friction doesn't mean going backward. It means coming back. Back to your body. Back to your attention. Back to the part of you that knows how to decide. The reason this feels freeing over time is because agency is regulating. The brain relaxes when it trusts that *you* are in charge. Not the red dot. Not the feed. Not the algorithm anticipating your next itch.

At first, friction feels like effort. Then it feels like space. Eventually, it feels like relief. Because freedom isn't the absence of constraint. It's the presence of choice. And every time you choose to pause instead of react, to sit instead of scroll, to stay instead of flee discomfort, you're not failing at modern life. You're reclaiming it.

This idea isn't coming from the margins. It's being acknowledged at the very center of modern technology. In a Stanford talk, Jensen Huang, the CEO of Nvidia, told students something striking: *"I wish upon you ample doses of pain and suffering."*

His point wasn't cruelty. It was capacity. He argued that greatness and character are forged through struggle, not just intelligence, and warned that high expectations paired with constant ease tend to produce low resilience.

What he was naming is the same paradox at the heart of our digital lives. We've built systems that eliminate friction at every turn while quietly wondering why our tolerance for difficulty, boredom, and uncertainty is disappearing. We've optimized for speed, convenience, and instant relief, then act surprised at the erosion of patience, depth, and perseverance.

Innovation doesn't come from constant comfort. Neither does emotional resilience. When relief is always one tap away, the nervous system never learns how to settle itself. When discomfort is immediately outsourced to distraction, the muscles of agency weaken. What feels like kindness in the short term—removing every obstacle—becomes fragility over time.

This is why friction matters. Not as punishment, but as preparation. Not as suffering for its own sake, but as the space where choice, regulation, and self-trust are built. Without it, we don't become more efficient humans—we become more dependent ones.

AWKWARD SILENCE

In Tulum, I thought silence would bring clarity. It only brought chaos.

My idea: Go on an eighteen-day trip to write my second book, *Reclaim* (yes, this book). I was on a one-month paid sabbatical, a luxury reserved for employees who had worked five years at the company—Uber—but really a thank-you to those who didn't quit during the Great Resignation. After a breakup months earlier, I wanted to get away. Unplug. So I booked the flight and three different honeymoon-worthy hotels. If not the guy, then at least the trip.

If you're unfamiliar with Tulum, think of it as Cabo's hippie cousin. Three hours south of Cancun, it looks very different from the large luxury resorts of Baja's crown jewel. Instead, there's a dirt road along the beach packed with tourists and taxis. The buzz of generators can be heard as the jungle plays host to digital junkies too busy to put their phones down and look up, even though they've chosen a destination where Wi-Fi is limited and TVs are nonexistent. Visitors are, as usual, more eager to capture their perfect photos than to experience the present moment. As someone who used to wear a button on her college backpack that said *Kill Your TV,* I was ready. Or so I thought.

The red flags started before I even arrived. As I began packing, I started doing something unusual: collecting activities and spending money on physical items "to keep me entertained." Looking back, it was anxiety, the preemptive fear of being alone, with no stimulation in sight.

I planned to go completely off the grid so I could spend my days relaxing and writing by the pool. I told my parents and provided them with my itinerary, along with the contact information for each hotel in case they needed to get in touch with me.

The truth is, I never turned my phone off, not once.

Why? For starters, the idea of being disconnected while alone in a jungle in a foreign country didn't sit right with me. My intuition was screaming, *Absolutely not.* I didn't feel safe unplugging: ground-floor room, broken lock, phone on one side of my pillow, my purple pepper spray on the other.

I felt like a fraud. Here I was, trying to help others with digital well-being, and I couldn't even do twenty-four hours without my phone. How was I going to make the most of the life-changing two weeks I had planned?

And who was I to write a book? That's the point: You don't write a book like this if you have it all figured out. You write it because you've been through it. The other issue: Even though the hotels were more hut than Hilton, technology still permeated the experience. Even basic tasks like ordering room service required an app. I kept my phone in the safe, but reaching for it felt like a hard-to-resist temptation.

I paced back and forth on my balcony, taking in the magical melody of the birds and the gentle tapping of an afternoon rain shower. All I could really think, though, was how cool this would be to record. I told myself, *Just one video—no internet.*

My mind raced. What was happening in the world? Cut off from the media only a day after one of the most divisive elections of our time. The guilt weighed heavily on my mind. I wasn't keeping up. I wasn't informed. When a group of foreign tourists laughed about the "clueless American," it stung more deeply than I had expected. I was irritable because I was detoxing, not from drugs or alcohol, but from technology. I was hot and sweaty, and not just from the Tulum humidity or the bed bugs I picked up at my second hotel.

Every minor discomfort was amplified. The hum of the generator, the grit of sand in the sheets, the silence so quiet that your thoughts feel like a scream. I wasn't relaxed; I was restless. If you've ever felt that "itch" in the silence, you know what I'm talking about.

Only later did I understand what was happening. Friedrich Nietzsche, a nineteenth-century German philosopher, wrote obsessively about what it means to become strong in a world that prefers comfort. He believed that growth doesn't come from ease or reassurance, but from discomfort and solitude—the kind that strips away distraction and forces you to confront yourself without an audience.

In Nietzsche's view, silence isn't peaceful at first, because it exposes what noise usually numbs. And, like any unused muscle, it aches when you finally engage it. That's why it felt like withdrawal. Because it is. But that discomfort isn't a flaw—it's a doorway. You ask yourself: *How did I get here? Why does silence feel so terrifying? Is there something wrong with me?*

The truth is nothing is wrong with you. You're not broken. You're detoxing from a world that never stops. I didn't emerge calm or enlightened. Nothing resolved neatly. But there were small moments. Minutes when I didn't reach for my phone. An afternoon when the restlessness softened just enough to notice the light shifting across the floor. The silence didn't become peaceful, but it stopped feeling hostile. That was the doorway.

Not relief. Not clarity. Just the absence of panic where panic used to live.

I didn't want this lesson. The silence stripped me down and showed me what I was hiding from. What I learned in Tulum is that restlessness isn't a sign of failure.

It's the first sign of healing.

part ii

the needs our tech meets

RECLAIM

THE DIGITAL REFRAME

I found what I had been missing on a spring morning in California. The kind of morning that feels like the world is showing off—jasmine in the air, coastal dew still clinging to everything, white egrets gliding slowly and unhurriedly through the morning sun. Brisk and alive. I wasn't doing anything remarkable. I was just there, and, for once, so was my mind.

That's what attention feels like when it's not being pulled. Not dramatic. Just present.

There were nights writing this book when I'd close my laptop at 2 a.m., eyes burning, and let my mind drift somewhere else entirely. Not to sleep, but to a version of my life that felt further and further away. Poolside with a book. At the river with my dog. A picnic where the only thing passing the time was sunshine and the sound of birds. No notifications. No deadlines.

I'd catch myself daydreaming about going back to basics, back to the sounds that don't demand anything from you, back to days that don't have to be optimized or documented or proven.

Then I'd open my laptop again.

The irony wasn't lost on me. Here I was, writing about reclaiming your life from technology, while my own life had never felt more consumed by it. The edit turnarounds, the late weekends, the pressure to produce. I was deep in it. Somewhere underneath all of it was a quieter version of me, the one who still wished she could return to something simpler, before technology started making so many demands on what it means to just be a person.

I told myself, *It's just for now.* But I knew that voice. I'd heard it before.

We've been told that the antidote is to "detox." Delete the apps, escape for a long weekend, or go on a digital fast. But detoxing isn't a sustainable solution; it's a temporary one. You always come back. And when you do, the environment that overwhelmed you hasn't changed.

It's like drying off with the same dirty old towel.

Digital detoxes also reveal privilege, unavailable to the single parent relying on apps to coordinate childcare. Or the hourly worker whose schedule lives in a group chat. The student whose entire coursework runs through a portal. The person whose only connection to family is a phone screen and a time-zone difference.

For them, a digital detox isn't a wellness practice. It's a threat to the life they've built around staying connected. Even for those who can step away, detoxing doesn't teach awareness. It teaches avoidance. You come back to the same person, to the same environment, with the same habits. Just slightly more rested.

I tried the other ones first. I used products like Brick to block my phone, but quickly learned that the tool only works if you *use* it. I'd go two weeks strong, under an hour a day, then Sunday night would happen. A binge that left me feeling like it was all lost. But I'd decide to start over again the next morning.

That ebb and flow taught me more than any detox ever did. I started telling people about it, not to shame myself into compliance, but because sharing the journey made it feel less like a failure and more like a practice. That's the difference between curiosity and fear. Fear makes you quit. Curiosity makes you try again.

Technology is not your enemy. It's a mirror reflecting your patterns, priorities, and pain points. When you open your phone, you open a reflection of your habits: who you follow, what you click, and where your attention goes when you're tired or anxious.

The goal isn't to smash the mirror. It's to clean it.

A digital reframe invites us to view technology not as a threat, but as a tool for transformation. It challenges the myth that control means disconnection. It gives us permission to be both wired and well. Because this isn't about rejecting technology. It's about reclaiming ownership over how we use it.

When we reclaim our digital lives, we don't just transform ourselves, we change the digital culture to which we contribute. That's what Nicholas Christakis and James Fowler found in their large-scale research on social networks: that behaviors and emotions don't stay contained within individuals. They ripple outward, through networks, even without direct interaction.

I've watched it happen. A speech-writing coach told me our work together had changed how he saw his own habits—he noticed he was scrolling between calls instead of taking aligned action toward his sales goals to support his family. Our team's self-appointed TikTok queen put a limit on her favorite app. Students came back months later saying something had quietly shifted. Nobody made it a moment. It just traveled.

Every mindful click, every intentional post, every conscious boundary creates ripple effects. Not through grand gestures, but through quiet modeling. It shows others, especially the next generation, that presence is still possible in a hyperconnected world.

Technology will always evolve. But so can your relationship with it.

The digital reframe is about stepping out of default mode and remembering that you are the designer of your own attention. You don't have to live by the algorithm. You can choose to live in alignment with your values.

You're not just curating your feed.

You're modeling what's normal.

ATTENTION DIALS

If the digital reframe is an invitation to step out of default mode, the next realization is quieter—and more disarming.

You don't lose attention. You adjust it.

We talk about focus like it's a switch—on or off, present or gone. But attention doesn't vanish. It relocates. And the body makes that decision long before the mind catches up, responding to signals we don't consciously register: the tightness in your chest when an email sits unanswered, the flatness in the air when you're alone too long, the specific quality of silence that makes you reach unthinkingly for your phone.

Stress tightens attention into a pinpoint. Curiosity opens it. Fatigue blurs the edges. Safety lets it soften and settle. Most of the time, attention isn't missing—it's been quietly reassigned to whatever promises relief. A scroll. A refresh. A check. The shift happens so smoothly, you don't notice you've moved until you're twenty minutes deep into something you didn't mean to start. That's when the voice arrives. *Why can't I just stop? What's wrong with me?*

Attention isn't misbehavior. It's a messenger.

We want to believe we're one person—one will, one set of values, one steady hand on the wheel. But we're not. We're more like a family at Thanksgiving dinner. Different parts of us show up depending on what's happening in the moment. There's the part that keeps talking just to fill any silence—the one that needs stimulation when the world goes flat. The part that watches the door, monitoring for connection, because silence can start to feel like abandonment. The part that slips away to the kitchen when feelings get too loud to hold. And the part that scrolls not to find anything, but to avoid feeling what's already at the table.

These parts aren't broken. They're old strategies that worked once—maybe when you were young, maybe when things were harder—and now they're still running the same program, trying to keep you safe the only way they know how. Technology doesn't create these patterns. It just responds to them faster than anything else can.

Some of those patterns were trained at a desk long before you had a problem. One screen permitted, everything else not. You were doing exactly what was expected. Following the rules. Being professional. Nobody called it conditioning, but that's what it was.

Technology is exceptionally good at giving us what we *want*—and most of us never learned to tell the difference between a want and a need. Wants are urgent. Immediate. They arrive with a demand: *Give me something right now.* Needs are quieter. Slower. They whisper underneath, *Help me feel steady enough to stay.*

Tech delivers wants on demand—novelty, validation, distraction, escape—all of it instant, all of it compelling. But what the body needs runs deeper: reassurance that you're not alone, grounding when everything feels too fast, rest that doesn't require performing. The felt sense that you're allowed to take up space without earning it. So we keep reaching, hoping the next notification or scroll or click will finally land us somewhere that feels like enough.

Sometimes we don't even want what we're checking for. We just need the act of checking. The movement itself. The reassurance that something *could* be there, even when there isn't. You open the app, close it, open it again—not because you missed anything, but because stillness hasn't landed yet.

This is regulation masquerading as reaching.

It's like standing in a hallway with your hand on a door handle, opening it just to make sure it still opens, then closing it again. Not to leave. Not because you expect something new on the other side. Just to reassure yourself that you could.

But attention isn't a door you either walk through or leave closed.

It's a dial.

I do some of my clearest thinking on the couch with my laptop balanced on my knees and a familiar Netflix show playing in the background—not because I'm distracted, but because I'm regulated. The murmur of voices. The glow of the screen. That kind of ambient company. From the outside, it probably looks scattered. Inside, it's the exact calibration my nervous system needs to drop its guard long enough for ideas to surface. The attention isn't lost. It's tuned to the frequency at which thinking becomes possible.

This is what most people miss: Our attention habits aren't random. They're archaeological. Layers of old learning about how to stay safe, stay close, stay in control when the ground felt unstable. Some of us learned early on that staying hypervigilant meant staying connected, so now we check our phones like we're monitoring for danger. Others learned that disappearing was safer than being seen, so now we scroll to vanish.

These patterns don't announce themselves. They just run silently in the background, tuning the dial toward what feels familiar, even when it's become a cage.

When safety drops, attention narrows to the width of a thread. When safety returns, the world gets wider. Choice comes back online. You can't discipline your way out of dysregulation. This is why willpower never works. Restraint only lands when regulation comes first.

I learned this from a boss who sent valentines to her whole team and started every meeting with an icebreaker delivered with a warmth that made hard conversations feel safe.

One day, she sat me down after a difficult situation. Not to talk about what had happened, but about how I had responded. She wasn't criticizing me. She was handing me something. Your reaction, she said, is yours. Not the circumstance. Not the other person. Not the outcome. Just the reaction. That's the only place your power lives.

It stayed with me. Not just as career advice, but as something truer—that emotions aren't weaknesses to manage around. They're needs, asking to be understood.

Once I started treating them that way, everything got clearer. The reaching for my phone. The anxiety about being offline. The compulsion to check. None of it was random. It was need, looking for the fastest available response.

Nearly two thousand years ago, a Stoic philosopher named Epictetus taught his students that freedom doesn't come from controlling everything—it comes from knowing what's yours to control, and releasing everything else. You don't control the weather. You don't control other people. You don't control the chaos of the world. But you *do* control where you place your attention, your effort, your care. That distinction—between what's yours and what isn't—is where peace lives.

Entrepreneur Ramit Sethi has spent the better part of two decades teaching personal finance to millions of people, and his most radical idea has nothing to do with budgets or spreadsheets. It isn't about cutting lattes or tracking every dollar or learning to feel guilty about what you spend. It's simpler than that, and stranger than that, and most people in the personal finance world aren't saying it.

It's about dials.

The premise starts with a question most people never ask. Not, "How do I spend less?" but, "What matters to me?" Those are different questions, and they lead to completely different lives. The first one shrinks your life. The second forces you to define it. Ramit's argument is that most people are so focused on the first question that they never get around to the second, and so they spend their whole lives optimizing for discipline instead of meaning.

Here's the confronting part. Most people don't have a spending problem. They have a decision problem. They're unconsciously funding a life they never chose, built from habit, from inertia, from other people's expectations of what a responsible adult is supposed to want.

Sethi calls them money dials. Everyone has a small number of areas that bring them disproportionate joy or meaning. Not everything. A few things. For one person, it's travel. For another it's food, or fitness, or the quality of their home. The category doesn't matter. What matters is that it's genuinely yours, not inherited from someone else's idea of what a good life looks like.

As Ramit puts it, "Spend extravagantly on the things you love, and cut costs mercilessly on the things you don't." Not moderately. Not responsibly. Extravagantly on one end, mercilessly on the other.

The pattern he sees is almost always the same. A couple is feeling financially squeezed despite earning what should be enough. When you look at where the money is going, the problem isn't income. It's misalignment. They're spending across dozens of categories that don't genuinely matter to them. Not because they chose them. Because they never stopped to question them. Subscriptions they forgot about, upgrades that seemed like the adult thing to do, habits picked up from parents or roommates or ambient pressure about what you're supposed to want.

In one case, a couple realized that dining out—which consumed a significant chunk of their monthly spending—wasn't something they particularly valued. They did it out of habit, out of convenience, out of never having decided otherwise. What they loved was travel. Long trips, new places, the feeling of being somewhere completely different. They weren't doing much of it because it felt like too big an expense. But they were spending thousands of dollars a year on dinners they barely remembered.

They redirected the money. Cut the dining, put it toward travel. Same income. Same city. Same jobs. Completely different experience of their life.

Nothing about their discipline changed. Their clarity did.

That's what Ramit keeps coming back to. The goal was never control. It was alignment. The people who transform their financial lives don't suddenly become more virtuous. They get honest about what they want, then stop spending on everything else.

The relief surprises people every time. They expect the conversation about cutting back to feel like deprivation. What they feel instead is permission. Permission to stop performing a version of adulthood they never questioned. Permission to stop funding a life that looks right from the outside but feels strangely hollow from the inside. And maybe, for the first time, permission to ask what they want, then build toward that instead.

The goal was never less.

It was right.

And money isn't the only place this shows up. It's just the easiest place to see it.

Epictetus would recognize this immediately. Different century, same truth: You don't need control over everything. You need clarity about what's yours.

You don't control the feed. You don't control the algorithm, the notification design, the infinite scroll, or what anyone else does with their screen time. You don't control how fast the digital world spins or how hard it pulls.

But you *do* control the dial. How much access it gets. How much space it takes. How loud the signal needs to be for you to feel steady. How much of your inner life you hand over in exchange for the promise of something that might—maybe—finally feel like enough.

Once you see what's turning the dial—once you understand what your attention is responding to, what it's trying to solve, why it keeps circling back to the same digital spaces—the question changes shape entirely.

It stops being "*Should I quit?*" and becomes, "*How much is enough right now?*"

Not forever. Not as a moral position or a productivity hack. Just right now—today, this week, this season of your life, given what you know about yourself and what your body is requesting.

That's not restriction. That's tuning.

That's where the dials come in.

RED. YELLOW. GREEN.

Once you understand attention as a dial, not a switch, the question stops being, "*Should I quit technology*?" and becomes something far more usable: *"How much access does this deserve right now?"* This is where Red, Yellow, and Green come in. They aren't judgments. They aren't promises you make to be better tomorrow. They're settings.

Red: The default is running you.

Yellow: You're starting to notice.

Green: You're choosing.

You don't have to aim for green every day. You just have to know which setting you're in, and adjust from there. The same behavior can be Red one day and Yellow the next, not because you're inconsistent, but because you're responsive.

The goal isn't to renegotiate your entire digital life every day. Most people do better with defaults. Workdays need different boundaries than weekends. Heavy seasons need different inputs than lighter ones. Then you adjust when something stops working, not from scratch, but from awareness. That's what makes it sustainable.

You don't control the feed. You don't control the algorithm.

But you do control the setting.

That's not avoidance. That's agency.

None of the settings are fixed. What's Green one day might be Yellow the next. What's Yellow under calm conditions might need to be Red under stress. The same app can regulate one part of you and overwhelm another. The same behavior can support you in one season and erode you in another.

That doesn't mean you're inconsistent. It means you're responsive.

The goal isn't to live in Green all the time. The goal is to notice when the dial needs adjusting and to trust yourself enough to turn it. That's the work. And once you know how to tune the dial, the next question becomes inevitable:

If not this, then what?

Enter the RECLAIM Method.

WHAT THIS COSTS

Before we talk about what to do, I want to name what unchecked technology use has cost us. Not in hours. In something harder to measure and harder to get back.

The cost isn't just lost time. Lost time is the easiest part to see. What's harder to see, and what took me longer to reckon with, is what repeated leaving does to a person over years.

It makes you worse at being present. Not dramatically, not all at once, but incrementally, in the way that anything practiced becomes second nature. Every time I left a conversation to check something, I was practicing leaving. Every time I filled a quiet moment before it had a chance to become anything, I was practicing avoidance. Every time I chose the frictionless exit over the harder feeling, I was practicing the choice. Until the choice stopped feeling like a choice at all.

That's the loop. Not an app, not a notification, not a bad habit with a simple fix. A loop, automatic and invisible and self-reinforcing, running in the background of your actual life.

Then, one day, you look up and realize you can't remember the last time you sat with someone and were fully there. You can't remember the last time boredom became curiosity instead of a problem to solve. You can't remember the last time you had a thought that wasn't interrupted. Not because something dramatic happened. Because you practiced your way out of it, one small exit at a time.

That's what this is really about. Not screen time. Not productivity. Not digital wellness as a lifestyle category. It's about what kind of person you're quietly becoming every time you reach without choosing.

I didn't realize it at the time, but I was building a system, one I now call the RECLAIM Method. Most people think they have an attention problem. They don't. They're stuck in a loop. The RECLAIM Method is how you break it.

It's not a program. It's not a detox. It's a sequence—seven stages that move you from unconscious reaching to deliberate living. You don't have to do them in order. You don't have to do them all at once. But if something isn't sticking, it's almost always because one of the seven is missing.

R: RECOGNIZE

Nothing changes before this. The loop closes fastest in the dark of nonrecognition. When you can't see what's driving the reach, you can't interrupt it.

Your phone use isn't random. It has a shape; a schedule, almost. It's not weakness. It's wiring. And wiring can be changed.

I noticed it one night when I put my phone down and couldn't recall a single thing I'd seen. Not one post, not one idea, nothing worth keeping. Twenty minutes, gone.

I was telling myself I was staying informed. Staying connected. When I looked honestly, I wasn't connected to anything. I was leaving. Over and over, choosing to leave whatever I was actually in—a conversation, a thought, a room with people I loved—because somewhere else felt easier than here.

Before anything changed, the story had to crack. Not my habits, not my screen time. The *story.* The puffed-up one I'd been telling myself about what I was doing and why.

One question cracked it: Why now? Why my phone, at this moment? The pause this creates is maybe two seconds. In those two seconds, something invisible becomes visible. I was avoiding something. I was bored. I didn't want to be alone with whatever was sitting in the room with me. I might still unlock it. But now I'm *choosing,* instead of just moving.

In her book *How to Break Up with Your Phone,* Catherine Price describes three ways we spend our time online: connection, creation, and consumption. Two of them are genuinely good. Connecting with people we care about. Creating something meaningful. But when I held that framework up against my actual behavior—without adjusting the answer to make myself feel better—the picture became very clear, very fast. Almost everything pulling me back was the third category. Not intentional consumption. The automatic kind. The kind I did for twenty minutes and had absolutely nothing to show for.

We weren't consuming content. We were consuming our lives and calling it staying informed.

I reached for my phone at the same moments, for the same reasons, every single day. When I felt stuck. When something got hard. When I didn't know what to do next. When something visited me that I didn't want to feel.

When I started teaching this to students, one of them stopped me after a session and said something I haven't forgotten: *"I realized that half the time, I didn't even want to be on my phone."*

That's it. That's the whole recognition. Not a dramatic transformation. Just a two-second pause that made the invisible visible.

The behavior was never the problem. The moment before it was.

E: EXIT THE LOOP

Seeing the loop isn't enough. You need a way out before it closes.

German "spiritual teacher" and self-help author Eckhart Tolle calls it "the one conscious breath"—meditation stripped to its minimum, available anywhere, costing nothing.

My story with presence didn't start on a Google bus or a philosophy dissertation. It started in the transfer dorms at Chico State during winter break, when almost everyone else had gone home. I was eighteen. A freshman who had moved in mid-year, which means you arrive to empty hallways and a quiet that makes you feel like you've missed something. I remember seeing a guy across the common area and running out to say hi, not because I knew him, but because something in me just did.

What he lacked in height, he made up in everything else. A rugby scrum half, which tells you something: small and explosive, the one who holds the whole formation together. Smart. Social. Athletic and genuinely, effortlessly himself—the kind of person who never seemed to be performing anything. He was the son of the dean of Santa Clara Law, which meant a certain future had been quietly arranged for him. He chose forest-service work. He chose a state school and a degree in health care administration instead. He chose the life that called him over the one that waited.

He was my first love. The full package, and I was just too young, too unformed, to hold it.

But here's what he gave me that I've carried ever since: He noticed something I didn't have language for yet. That I was never quite where I was. Always rehashing the past or rehearsing the future, my anxiety running like a background system I couldn't close. He didn't diagnose it or lecture me. He just handed me a book.

Eckhart Tolle's *The Power of Now*.

I didn't understand all of it the first time. But I understood enough. The idea that the present moment is the only place where life happens—not in the memory of what was or the anticipation of what might be, but here, now, this—landed somewhere deep, and stayed.

He was the one who got away. But what he left behind became the heart of everything I've built since. That one conscious breath Tolle describes—I'd been taught it before I had the words for it. The pause between impulse and action. The space where you remember you have a choice.

A second decision works the same way. When the app closes, reopening it requires a choice. And that choice breaks the spell.

Distraction doesn't feel like escape. It feels like necessity.

I'd be in the middle of something hard, and my thumb was already moving before I'd made a decision. It's a trained reflex—every time I let it fire, I was further teaching myself something that took a long time to unteach. I started avoiding things before they began, because in the back of my mind, I already knew how it ended: with me, leaving.

The phone hadn't done that to me. I had, by reaching for it every time something felt hard.

When the impulse fires: *Not yet*. Give yourself enough space between the impulse and the action to remember *you* are the one deciding. The first few times, the pause felt almost theatrical. I stayed in it anyway. Ten seconds. Twenty.

The urge passed—and on its own. No scroll, no distraction. Just gone. This is where the loop breaks, unable to reach over that two-second gap you created. Before unlocking your phone, count to five. Put the phone face down before you open it. Stand up, change rooms, change position. Your body moving breaks the reflex faster than your mind arguing with it.

I trusted myself to "just check for a minute" more times than I can count. It was never a minute. It was never even close. So I stopped relying on the version of me who would hopelessly overestimate her own willpower. I set limits. Not as punishment. As protection. When the app closed, it closed. Reopening it required a second decision. Sometimes I made it. More often I didn't, because the second decision broke the spell, and without the spell, there was nothing I wanted. I wasn't restricting myself. I was refusing to negotiate with myself in those moments when the outcome was already decided. The behavior I repeated most wasn't the one I wanted most. It was the one that cost least to reach.

My phone didn't win because it mattered more than everything else. It won because it was easier. No transition, no decision, no gap between impulse and action. I hadn't built a habit. I'd built a zero-resistance pipeline to the part of my brain that was always looking for an exit.

The fix wasn't wanting it less. It was slightly increasing the cost, just enough for a thought or two to intervene. Grayscale. Logged-out apps. Phone in another room during focused work. My hand reached, felt something unexpected as my brain reengaged for one second.

And that second was enough.

C: CHOOSE AGAIN

This is where agency returns. And where most people accidentally restart the loop.

I quit scrolling more times than I'll tell you. Each time, I thought I was finally being serious. Each time, I went back. I was using my phone to avoid sitting with who I was. Not occasionally—consistently. Every gap, every quiet moment, every feeling I didn't want to look at. I wasn't addicted to my phone. I was addicted to not having to feel whatever was true. The phone was just the most convenient exit I had.

Here's the thing nobody says plainly enough: The phone didn't create the avoidance. It just made it effortless. The feelings were always there. The discomfort was always there. The phone just meant I never had to develop any tolerance for either.

The scroll was the routine. What I was after was *relief.* Remove the routine without addressing the need, and the need finds another outlet. Most people restart the loop here without realizing it. Same exit, different door.

One question changed it: *What do I* need *right now?* Sometimes the answer was movement—a short walk, not a workout, just outside. Sometimes it was contact, a real text to one person instead of passively watching everyone else's lives. Sometimes it was water, or a stretch, or just two minutes standing in the kitchen doing nothing.

The first time I caught this impulse and instead did the smaller, truer thing, the feeling went away. Not numbed, not buried. Gone.

I realized, too, that it wasn't the big things I never started that bothered me. It was the small things I kept meaning to get back to. Like writing, or some version of my morning that felt possible—for a while, anyway. Eventually, I hadn't done these small things in so long that I stopped making promises to myself.

Any habit can start with a two-minute version of itself. When something feels too large, I avoid it before I've even tried. But you can make it small enough that avoidance can't get a foothold. Two minutes in, something shifts.

The resistance was never about the thing. It was about starting.

The question works in the moment. But moments are easier to win when the structure is already on your side. I spent a long time looking for room to start: a gap in the schedule, a morning that wasn't already claimed. It never came. But the structure was already there. I just kept looking past it. I make coffee every morning. I get into bed every night. These aren't decisions. They're grooves worn so deep, they don't register as choices.

The most durable place to attach something new is directly after something that already happens without asking. After the coffee, I stayed off my phone for ten minutes. After getting into bed, I read instead of scrolling.

One morning, the new habit just happened. Not because I remembered. Not because I pushed. Because it came after the coffee.

That's the whole method.

L: LIMIT THE DEFAULTS

By the time you're relying on willpower, you've already lost the advantage.

I mapped a single morning once, and it was mortifying. Reaching for my phone on the nightstand, before I'd even had a thought. Notification on every app. Every platform moving before I'd decided to move. I had genuinely believed I was bad at discipline. Turns out I was losing a game specifically designed for me to lose, then blaming myself for it.

I had been designed against, and I'd spent years calling it a personal flaw.

I stopped trying to fix me then, and changed the conditions: phone out of the bedroom. Apps deleted, browser only. Notifications off; not silenced, *off.* One extra step between me and everything that had been pulling without asking.

I kept telling myself I needed to use my phone less. That framing never worked. It felt vague, voluntary, easy to violate.

What worked was giving my usage a container—a temporary mental corral in which I could scroll and click without guilt. Not all day, not whenever the urge hit, but inside a limited framework. Twenty minutes in the afternoon. Twenty minutes at night. When I opened it during those windows, there was no guilt, no negotiation. When I reached for it outside of them, the question was simple: intentional or drifting?

Sometimes that was enough. Sometimes it wasn't. But it was always the right question.

My phone used to live everywhere: in my hand, on the table, face up beside my plate, always within reach, always on.

I gave it a place. A drawer. A counter. Another room.

The distance doesn't have to be dramatic.

It just has to be enough to break the body's automatic reach.

A: ACT YOUR WAY INTO A NEW IDENTITY

Tactics maintained by effort eventually fail. What holds long term isn't discipline. It's identity.

Managing yourself is exhausting. The constant negotiation, the quiet bargaining, the "just this once" that keeps resetting the clock. These are the sentences I started saying to myself, not as rules, but as identity statements. "I don't check my phone at dinner. I don't bring it into bed. I finish what I start. I stay in the room."

These are decisions, not rules. Rules get broken and forgiven and broken again, but decisions get lived. Saying one of those sentences out loud doesn't ask me to try harder. It asks me to stop being the version of myself that needed the rule in the first place.

The phone is still there. I'm just no longer someone who reaches for it unconsciously.

For a long time, I told myself I wasn't someone who followed through. I had enough evidence for that story, and I kept adding to it: every broken streak, every promise that didn't hold, every "just this once" that became twice.

So I stopped collecting evidence against myself.

I started noticing the small wins I'd been ignoring. The mornings I held the boundary. The moments I didn't reach. The decisions I made and kept. Not the transformations. The tiny, almost forgettable moments of doing what I said I would.

They didn't feel like much at the time. They never do. But they were adding up to something I hadn't had in years: *proof.* Not that I was perfect. That I was possible. That the version of me I kept describing in future tense was already showing up, quietly, in the present.

That's where it turns. Not in the big moments. In enough small ones that the story changes.

The pattern doesn't shift all at once. It shifts the next time you reach.

I: INTEGRATE INTO LIFE

Integration is what happens when the method stops being something you do and starts being how you live. This is what an ordinary Tuesday looks like when nothing is dramatic and the system either runs quietly or it doesn't.

Here's what it looked like, in practice, to find my way back.

My mornings used to disappear before they started. I'd wake up, reach for my phone, and within minutes I was inside someone else's urgency before I'd had a single thought of my own. So I made one change: no phone for the first thirty minutes of my day. I don't get it right every day. There are mornings I reach for it without thinking, telling myself I'm just checking something, and suddenly I'm ten minutes in before I've fully woken up. But on the mornings I don't reach, my thoughts feel calmer, more like mine.

I started sitting with myself for two minutes. No phone, no podcast, no task. Just sitting. It felt slow and uncomfortable and faintly ridiculous, like I was doing a bad impression of someone who meditates. Staying in it anyway was the whole practice. My thoughts came back, not pulled from a feed, not reactive—just mine. Now, every time I practice it, sitting with myself becomes slightly less like something I have to survive.

Most of my attempts at changing my behavior failed because I was the only one who knew about it. The decision was made alone, broken alone, and quietly restarted like nothing happened. It wasn't a discipline problem. It was a visibility problem. Telling one person changed it. Not publicly, not as a declaration. Just one person who would actually hear me. The moment it left my head and became real to someone else, it stopped being something I could quietly abandon. Tell one person what you're doing. Not as performance, just so it's real to someone besides yourself.

When I first tried to reduce my screen time, I focused on removing the behavior. Every time, I ended up right back where I started, because there was a gap and I hadn't decided what would fill it. Instead of removing the habit, I replaced it. A book on the nightstand. A notebook. A walk around the block. Nothing impressive, just something physical my hands could reach for that wasn't the phone. Meals without the phone on the table. Walks without it in my hand—not every walk, but some. The waiting room, the line at the coffee shop, the two minutes before a meeting starts; these used to be automatic scroll time. Now some of them are just *time.*

I still reach for my phone. Just as often now, I reach for something else.

My nights used to dissolve the same way my mornings did. One more check, one more scroll, until the day ended not with rest but with a slow fade I mistook for winding down. I drew a line at 9 p.m. After that point, nothing on my phone was something I needed. It was just something I was used to reaching for when I didn't know how to stop. The space it opened was quiet in a way I'd forgotten quiet could feel.

The same logic applies everywhere else. One thing at a time, start to finish. One person who knows what you're working on. One question before opening anything: *What am I here for?*

None of it is complicated. All of it compounds.

M: MAINTAIN AWARENESS

I still have off days. The difference now is they don't turn into lost weeks.

Each week I look once at my usage; not to punish myself, just to see. What got more of my time than I intended? Which apps gave something back, and which ones only cost? The audit takes five minutes. What it gives back is the sense of steering, rather than drifting.

There are still days I pick up my phone without deciding to. Still evenings that dissolve faster than I meant them to. The difference isn't perfection. It's that I notice sooner, and the noticing is enough to change what happens next.

The loop doesn't disappear. It goes quiet. And quiet isn't the same as gone. That knowledge doesn't disappear either. It just needs to be honored, in the small and ordinary way of someone who mostly chooses instead of drifts.

WHAT CHANGES

I want to be honest about what this does and doesn't do.

It doesn't make you someone who uses their phone less. It makes you someone who uses it differently, with some awareness of why, in ways that mostly give something back instead of just taking. Some days, that looks significant. Most days it looks like thirty minutes of quiet in the morning, a meal where I was in the room, a moment of boredom I sat with instead of immediately filling it with my feed.

That doesn't sound like much. Over time, those moments compounded into something I didn't expect: I started trusting myself again. I could be depended on. I was someone who did what she said she was going to do, who showed up for the things that mattered. Someone who mostly chooses instead of drifts.

What would it look like if you treated your own attention as something worth designing for, the same way you might design a morning, a workspace, a life?

I used to think I had an attention problem. I didn't. I had a practice problem.

You already know how to practice. You've been doing it for years.

You just haven't chosen what.

LIVING-ROOM EFFECT

Technology isn't neutral. It's an amplifier.

Your feed is more like your living room than you think. There's a lot you put there: the furniture, the photos, the things you chose. There's also dust, dog hair, books you left out. Things that accumulated without a decision. And even if you meticulously clean it up, that stuff will be back in a couple of weeks. The difference is you can see the dust in your living room. In your feed, it's almost invisible—and it's been quietly rearranging the furniture while you weren't looking.

That's the algorithm at work.

It doesn't just respond to your preferences. It responds to your activation. Outrage, fear, validation, curiosity, envy—whatever creates an emotional charge gets amplified. The system doesn't care what you believe. It cares what hooks you. You hesitate on a friend's vacation photo just long enough for the system to clock your envy. Next week, your feed is full of travel deals. Coincidence? Hardly.

A few years ago, my friend Sara went to Banff with her family. The photos were cinematic—the Fairmont below, the turquoise lake, and Sara in head-to-toe pink athleisure at the summit beside her Edward Cullen-look-alike twin brother.

I liked one photo, and for the next week, I was served both vacation packages and workout ads. It was clear the algorithm couldn't tell whether I wanted her trip or her triceps. That's when I realized the feed wasn't just showing me what I chose. It was amplifying what hooked me—even briefly.

Technology doesn't only amplify what we love. It amplifies what activates us. Political posts you never engaged with. Workout ads you never requested. Content from accounts you don't follow. The system isn't showing you what you want; it's showing you what keeps you looking.

You wake up and check your feed, only to realize that each day, it's showing a slightly smaller version of your world. With your every tap, click, and swipe, the algorithm refines what hooks you. Every micro-action tells the system what activates you.

Pause on a post about anxiety, and your feed tilts toward wellness content, even if you just liked the trending song. Laugh at an office meme, and workplace humor climbs your ranking score. You spend the next week binge-watching TikTok creator Sarai Marie, wishing you had the same courage as her character, Veronica, to combat toxic workplace culture. Scroll past politics, and your worldview narrows just a little more as you're relegated to reels that reinforce your beliefs.

The "shrinking self" is what happens when the algorithm starts to echo instead of expand you. The more it recognizes what hooks you, the more it reinforces it. Your feed becomes familiar and flattering, while quietly *flattening* who you could be.

What begins as personalization becomes limitation. Over time, you stop exploring—and you start echoing. The feed begins to amplify not who you are, but what activates you.

Agency is what turns that amplification into choice.

EASE

SUPPORT, NOT SUBSTITUTION

Going to the grocery store used to be one of my favorite things to do. Walking the aisles, deciding what sounded good, changing my mind halfway through. It felt like *being in* my life, a little luxury that ended with a bag full of my favorite things.

Then I got busy. Long days in recruiting. Interviews running before I woke up. By the time the day ended, I was done. So I started ordering. It felt like a trade at first. Save the hour. Be more productive. Then work perks at Uber covered the bill. Credits showed up, I ordered. Then it just became how things worked. I don't remember deciding to stop cooking. I only remember realizing I had.

I was living in a unit that overlooked the main walkway in our complex. Every day I watched delivery drivers come through. One after another. Bags in hand. Morning, afternoon, night. I was one of those orders. I hadn't decided to stop going to the store. I had just stopped. Somewhere in that process, I had handed off a small piece of my own life without noticing. It wasn't lost, nor was it fully there.

Growing up, I used to go to Target with my mom and wander the aisles for hours. No list. No plan. Just the two of us, moving through the store at whatever pace felt right, picking things up and putting them back, deciding together. It was never really about what we bought. It was about wandering, and the time together. Now I scroll Amazon reviews alone, with Netflix running in the background. Two screens at once, and neither one getting my full attention. I'm not shopping. I'm not watching. I'm doing both, badly, alone in the dark on the couch.

That's what quiet replacement looks like. Not a dramatic loss. Just the slow substitution of something shared and embodied for something efficient and solitary. The wandering became scrolling. My mom became a review algorithm. The aisle became a tab.

French philosopher Simone Weil once suggested that attention is the rarest and purest form of generosity we have. Not productivity. Not output. Attention. The simple, often effortful act of staying with something, or someone, without rushing past the situation at hand.

She wasn't talking about focus in the modern sense. She was talking about presence. About the way attention keeps us in relationship with the world instead of skimming across its surface. When attention is sustained, something deeper becomes possible: care, patience, responsibility, even love.

I know what it feels like when that presence disappears. Going to the store gives me anxiety now. The crowds, the decisions, the small talk at the checkout. There are days when delivery isn't laziness—it's survival. And I genuinely believe that for people who struggle with social anxiety, with sensory overwhelm, with bodies that make the world harder to move through, ease isn't a luxury. It's access.

But then I circle back to the uncomfortable question I can't stop asking myself: *Do I have social anxiety because I stopped going to the store? Or did I stop going to the store because I have social anxiety?* I'm not sure I know anymore. And I'm not sure I can unknot which came first.

Ease doesn't just respond to our limitations. It might be quietly creating them. Through repetition. Through the slow withdrawal of practice, until the thing you stopped doing starts to feel impossible.

Ease is one of the great promises of modern life, and one of its most misunderstood.

We're told ease will give us our lives back. More time. Less friction. Fewer decisions at the end of an already long day. And in many ways, it has. Grocery delivery means you don't have to spend your energy navigating fluorescent aisles after work. Medication delivery means you can care for yourself when you're sick and living alone.

So let's be clear: Ease itself isn't the problem. The problem is what happens when ease quietly becomes the default setting for life.

There's a phrase we've repeated for generations: "It takes a village." For most of human history, that wasn't a metaphor. It was how life worked. Needs were met through shared effort, shared knowledge, shared presence. Help came from people—neighbors, family, community—through relationships that required patience, coordination, and mutual reliance.

The village hasn't disappeared. It's been replaced. What once moved through people now moves through systems. Food arrives. Maps decide routes. Notifications remember. Medications show up at the door.

What matters is noticing the difference between support and substitution, and how quietly one can slide into the other. Support shows up when life is heavy. Substitution shows up so consistently that you stop noticing what you can handle on your own, or who you might turn to without something stepping in first.

What was once a choice became the environment. And environments shape us quietly.

Historically, friction wasn't seen as a flaw. It was formative. Walking to get food wasn't just a task; it was a way of life that valued movement, interaction, and anticipation. Waiting wasn't wasted time—it created space for reflection and emotional regulation. Asking for help was seen less as a weakness than how connection was sustained.

Friction didn't slow life down. It helped people feel it.

Ease changes how attention behaves. When life moves without requiring us, attention thins. Not because we're lazy or disengaged, but because there's less to stay *with*. When systems carry us through, our attention is freed, but it's also displaced.

That's the quiet tradeoff. Ease doesn't just remove effort; it removes opportunities for attention to land. And when attention doesn't land anywhere for long, our relationship to life becomes lighter, faster, less rooted. Ease can support attention, or it can quietly scatter it. The difference isn't in the technology. It's in whether ease leaves room for you to remain present in your own life.

When everything works automatically, we stop practicing. Not all at once. Gradually. Quietly. The skills friction once trained begin to fade—not just practical ones, but relational ones too. Asking. Waiting. Tolerating discomfort. This is the paradox: Ease can support a life. But when ease replaces effort and replaces connection, we slowly lose our sense of capability.

That loss doesn't feel alarming. It feels comfortable, efficient, even sensible. Until something small goes wrong, technology fails, plans change, life demands improvisation, and there's an uneasy feeling underneath. Less confidence. Less trust in your ability to respond without a system stepping in. That isn't a personal failing. It's a predictable outcome.

The goal here isn't to eliminate ease. It's to put it back in its proper place.

This is where reclaiming begins. Not by rejecting convenience, but by learning how to relate to it differently. The skill is knowing the difference between ease that serves you and ease that's become you.

YOUR EASE DIAL

Before you try to change anything, it helps to see where you are. As in what your normal, default day is like.

Red: Ease is running the show. Most things default to convenience without much thought. You order instead of decide. Check, instead of sit with uncertainty. Let systems handle small moments you used to move through yourself. Where you were once active, you're now more passive. Life feels efficient, but slightly distant—like everything is being handled, but you're not always the one handling it.

Yellow: You're starting to notice. You catch yourself mid-pattern. You recognize when you reach for what's easiest instead of what you actually want. Sometimes you interrupt it. Sometimes you don't. But the awareness is there. And once you see it, it's harder to ignore.

Green: You're using ease on purpose. You still use convenience. You're not trying to make life harder than it needs to be. But you choose when ease supports you, and when you want to stay involved. *You* decide. You stay present in the moments that matter. Ease works for you, not instead of you.

Where are you most of the time?

You don't need to fix it right now. Just see it clearly. That's where choice starts.

THE TIME ILLUSION

One of ease's most persuasive promises is that of time. It promises to give back time.

And often, it does—at least, on the surface. Ordering ahead means no waiting. Delivery reduces trips. Automation cuts down the number of tasks and decisions you have to carry through an already taxing day. In a world built around speed and responsiveness, saving time feels like relief.

But relief isn't the same as return.

The illusion isn't that ease fails to save time. It's that saved time automatically becomes lived time—that the minutes freed by convenience will somehow reappear as rest, connection, creativity, or meaning, without any further intention required.

What happens is quieter.

Time that's freed doesn't disappear. It gets reassigned—often immediately, often invisibly.

I started noticing this in small ways. I'd order groceries to save time, and while they were being unpacked, I'd check my phone "for a second." A meeting would end early, and instead of standing up or stepping outside, I'd scroll just to reset. I told myself it was a small reward—a guilty pleasure, my little treat during a busy day. An errand would disappear from my to-do list, and somehow that space would fill itself before I ever decided what I wanted to do with it.

Nothing intentional replaced the time. Something available did.

That's what surprised me most—not that the time vanished, but that it slipped away without resistance. The minutes didn't open into rest or creativity or presence. They dissolved into continuation.

One more tab.

One more message.

One more thing that felt harmless in isolation and left no trace once it was over. I wasn't doing anything "wrong." I was doing what came easiest in that environment.

Ease removes friction. And friction, for better or worse, used to be what ended things.

When you had to walk somewhere, the walk itself created a beginning and an end. When you had to wait, waiting created a pause. When effort was required, effort signaled completion. Convenience dissolves those boundaries. Activities bleed into one another, and endpoints soften. There's no clear moment where one thing finishes and another begins.

So time doesn't open—it fills, often with things that feel busy yet leave you strangely hollow.

This is why so many people feel both efficient and perpetually behind. Not because they're mismanaging time, but because time has become porous—easy to enter and easy to lose track of, but hard to reclaim once it's been absorbed.

The Time Illusion thrives in that softness. It convinces us that because something was faster, something meaningful must have been gained. But speed and direction aren't the same thing. Saving time doesn't answer the deeper question of what that time is for.

Reclaiming time isn't about doing less. It's about deciding what deserves your attention.

That decision is the skill. It's not about optimization or discipline, but *direction*. Without it, time defaults to the path of least resistance: the next notification, the next task, the next piece of content designed to meet you exactly where your attention already is. Ease clears space, but something always moves in to occupy it.

Here's where awareness turns from abstract idea to lived experience.

It begins by noticing what happens in the first few minutes after something "saves time." How quickly that space gets absorbed. Whether the time you gained feels like it gave you something back, or simply rolled into the next thing.

Reclaiming time doesn't require a dramatic overhaul. It starts by paying attention to where your time lands once it's been freed. Time doesn't disappear. It always ends up somewhere. And once you start seeing where it goes, you can't unsee it.

QUIET REPLACEMENT

Quiet replacement doesn't announce itself. It doesn't arrive as loss or failure or collapse. It arrives as help. As efficiency. As relief. That's what makes it so hard to notice.

The philosopher Ivan Illich warned about this decades ago. When systems grow powerful enough, they don't just assist human capacity. They replace it. Not through force. Through convenience. Through the quiet removal of effort.

What's taken isn't taken violently. It's taken lovingly.

One afternoon, I needed to pick a restaurant. Not a meaningful decision. Not a hard one. But I opened the app before I even had a thought. Thai. Salad. Pizza. I hadn't decided what I wanted. The app had decided what to serve me: A deal popped up for pepperoni pizza, and I clicked it. I wasn't choosing anymore. I was confirming.

That's what quiet replacement looks like. Skills don't disappear because we lose them. They fade because something else has been doing them for us, so smoothly we don't notice they've gone dormant. Judgment. Patience. Discernment. The ability to sit with uncertainty without immediately filling it. These aren't soft skills. They're survival skills. And they weaken when they're no longer required.

This is where reclaiming becomes practical. The solution isn't to reject systems or fetishize effort. It's not about doing everything the hard way or withdrawing from modern life. It's about noticing where ease is supporting you, and where it's quietly standing in for capacities you still want to inhabit yourself.

Some days, that looks like closing the app and just deciding. Sitting with *not knowing* instead of reaching for an answer. Taking the route without instructions, even once, just to remember your sense of direction still works. Letting discomfort exist long enough to remember you can hold it. Not to prove anything. Just to still be someone who shows up when the systems don't.

What we don't practice, we lose. Even when it's taken lovingly.

Ways to Stay in the Driver's Seat... So ease *supports* your life, instead of replacing it.

You don't need to remove convenience. You just need to stay involved.

Notice where things are happening for you, and where they're happening instead of you. Where decisions are being made before you make them. Where something steps in so quickly, you don't even feel the moment you used to fully inhabit.

Stay with those moments. Not to make life harder. Just to remember that you're still the one choosing it. Because the goal was never to do everything yourself. It was to remain someone who can. At best, that's what ease protects. And what ease quietly takes when left unexamined.

It's the sense that the life you're living is one you're actually in.

DISTRACTION

—

I was lying on the floor of the emergency room at Marin General—alone. My hands had begun to seize, and my body was cramping so violently, I couldn't control it. It was the sickest I'd ever been.

A reaction to a GLP-1 had left me severely dehydrated, but what I remember most is how ordinary it had all seemed. A single injection. One that half the people I knew were taking without a second thought. The kind of thing people talked about over brunch, traded tips about in group texts, and mentioned casually between meetings. Yet there I was, on an emergency room floor, wondering how something so normal had gone so wrong.

My neighbor had heard me getting sick through the walls and called 911 at 6 a.m. after my forty-eight hours of nonstop vomiting, alone, until my body had nothing left. The firefighters who responded were kind in the way that only people who show up for strangers in their worst moments can be. I will never forget that.

There are times I'm genuinely grateful for the internet. Truly. No irony.

By the time I was in that hospital bed, it was just me and the clock on the wall, and the clock was the enemy. So I did what most of us do. I picked up my phone. Just to have somewhere to put my eyes that wasn't the ceiling.

I scrolled through videos of people talking directly into their cameras—faces, voices, presence without obligation. It made me feel less alone in a room where I was very much alone. I moved from video to video, then into Yahoo News, reading article after article until I felt like I'd consumed the entire internet and looped back around to do it again. The dopamine hits kept coming, each one just enough to get me to the next thing.

Then there was ChatGPT—my collaborator, my *yes* in a moment when I needed confidence, my sounding board when I needed clarity. It sat there with me for hours, patient and present. I'd type a thought, get a response, feel slightly less adrift. Then do it again. It wasn't connection, exactly, but it was somewhere to put myself when I had nowhere else to go.

Until finally they gave me something for the pain, and I fell asleep with my phone still in my hand.

That night, the internet wasn't the problem. It was the only thing I had.

That's the part we never talk about. Distraction isn't always the enemy. Sometimes it's the thing that gets you through.

As a university recruiter, I showed up wherever students would let me in. Not just career fairs and polished info sessions. Smaller study rooms. Dorms. The places where people actually lived.

This one started with an international student I met through Girls Who Code, who happened to be a residential advisor. She reached out and asked if I'd come speak to her community—an undergraduate dorm around the corner from Telegraph Avenue.

When I stepped into the elevator at David Blackwell Hall, I saw a flier taped to the wall with my picture on it. A simple printout that meant someone had made space for this to happen.

About forty students showed up for Friday night pizza, so the room had that familiar mix. Some people leaning in, some just there for a slice. One girl in the middle row looked like she might fall asleep. Halfway through, I asked everyone to take out their phones and check their screen time for that day. A few numbers started coming out. Six. Eight. Someone said nine. Then, from the middle of the room: "Eleven." It was the girl who looked like she might fall asleep.

Then she said it again, like she didn't believe it herself.

Eleven hours.

I blinked. *I haven't even been* awake *for eleven hours,* I thought.

She looked down at her phone, then back up at the screen. Visibly stunned. And something shifted. The room grew still and quiet in a different way. Everyone had seen their own number.

But hearing that number aloud landed differently.

That's the moment the regulator framework was built for. Less to fix something than to name what was already happening so loudly in that room that a girl who looked like she might fall asleep was suddenly the most awake person there.

HOW WE COPE

Your habits aren't random. They're responsive.

If technology magnifies what hooks you, then every scroll, every check, every refresh is doing emotional work. Usually quietly, and almost always automatically.

Here's the thing most people miss: We don't reach for our phones because we lack discipline. We reach for them because something inside needs regulating. Maybe it's safety. Maybe it's relief. Belonging. Certainty. The feeling of being seen. Or just the simple comfort of knowing what comes next.

Think about the last time you picked up your phone without deciding to. What were you feeling right before? Bored? Anxious? Restless? Lonely? Overstimulated?

That feeling—that's the signal. The phone is just the response. Regulation isn't the enemy of agency; it's the doorway back to it.

We've been taught to see phone use as the problem. But the phone is the solution to something deeper that's asking for attention. And until you know what that something is, you'll keep reaching for the same tools, wondering why willpower never sticks.

We don't reach for our phones randomly. We reach for them the way we reach for anything that has ever made us feel better—out of habit, out of need, out of a particular discomfort we've learned to soothe a certain way.

Most people have a pattern. Not a flaw. A pattern. Something that developed for a reason and has been running quietly ever since.

Once you understand what a habit is regulating, it stops being a mystery. It stops running the show. That's when awareness turns into choice.

And that starts with understanding what you're reaching for.

See if you recognize yourself in any of these digital regulators.

A WATCHER: SOMEONE WHO REGULATES THROUGH INFORMATION

"If I stay informed, I'll stay safe."

Some mornings, the phone is in your hand before your feet hit the floor. Before coffee. Before you've said a word to yourself. You're scrolling headlines, not because something happened, but because it *might* have. And if it did, you want to know first.

You tell yourself it's just staying informed. But if you're honest, it feels less like curiosity and more like bracing.

It's not really about the news. It's the feeling that if something bad is coming, at least you'll see it first. You grew up needing to read the room. Unpredictability wasn't abstract; it was personal. So you learned to scan. And now you do it automatically, even when nothing's wrong.

Information isn't safety. Presence is.

If this is you, try checking once, at a set time, then ask: *Did I need this to get through my day?* Keep your phone across the room until that window. Remove news apps from your home screen so checking requires a decision, not a reflex. Replace the morning scroll with something physical first—feet on the floor, water, one breath before the phone.

And before opening anything: *Is something happening right now that requires my attention?*

A SCOREKEEPER: SOMEONE WHO REGULATES THROUGH SPORTS

"I want intensity without personal stakes."

You're refreshing the score during dinner. Checking the injury report while you're supposed to be in a meeting. You care more about a trade deadline than a decision you've been putting off in your own life.

It sounds like avoidance, but it's not quite that. Sports give you something most of life doesn't: clear rules, clean outcomes, a winner by the end of the night. When you're carrying decision fatigue or emotional weight that doesn't have an obvious resolution, your nervous system wants to put it somewhere. Sports offer a container.

The question isn't whether this is bad. It's whether you're using the box or hiding in it.

If this is you, here's what tends to help.

Watch the game. Skip the compulsive in-between checking. Live viewing with intention is different from the scroll. Give your fantasy or stats habit a specific window—Sunday mornings, for example—instead of letting it graze throughout the week. When you notice you're reaching for scores during a stressful moment, try naming it out loud: *I'm overwhelmed, and I want a clean outcome right now.*

And when you can, channel that same energy somewhere with real stakes—a physical challenge, a game with people you know.

A COMPANION: SOMEONE WHO REGULATES THROUGH NOISE

"I don't want silence."

You're not really watching. The video is just on. The same creator's voice in the background while you cook, while you get ready, sometimes while you fall asleep. You've probably replayed certain videos more than you'd admit, simply because they're familiar. Because silence, for you, is a little too loud.

This isn't about screen addiction. It's about company. Parasocial connection gives you presence without obligation: no need to respond, no emotional labor, no one who needs anything from you. For someone who spends a lot of time in their own head, who carries a lot for other people, that's not nothing.

But the thoughts waiting underneath the noise don't go anywhere. They just wait.

If this is you, here's what tends to help.

Try swapping background YouTube for music or a podcast with a natural end point—something that stops on its own, instead of autoplaying into the next thing. Build a short list of playlists or channels you return to intentionally. Choose the noise instead of defaulting to it. Once a day, try twenty minutes of silence—not as discipline, but just to hear what's underneath.

And when the urge to turn something on feels strongest, ask yourself honestly: *Am I lonely right now? Is there an actual person I could reach out to instead?*

AN ESCAPIST: SOMEONE WHO REGULATES THROUGH BINGEING TV

"I need everything to stop for a while."

You've seen it before. You know how it ends. And that's exactly the point.

There's something specific about rewatching a beloved show. *Grace and Frankie*, the original *Gossip Girl*, whatever your version is. You're not looking for something new. You're going somewhere safe. You already know these people. You know who ends up with whom, which episode gets hard, when it's okay to look away. When everything else feels like too much, familiarity is its own kind of rest.

You're probably over-functioning in your regular life. Carrying a lot for other people. Managing things no one sees. A rewatch is your nervous system asking for somewhere stable to land.

The only question worth asking: *Am I resting or disappearing?*

If this is you, here's what tends to help.

Decide on an episode limit before you start. Two is rest, five is escape, and your body usually knows the difference. Keep a short comfort list you return to intentionally, rather than scrolling endlessly through options when you're already depleted.

And, after a long binge, ask yourself honestly and compassionately: *What was I trying to not feel?*

A REASSURER: SOMEONE WHO REGULATES THROUGH CONSTANT CONTACT

"Connection keeps me steady."

You sent the message. Now you're staring at *Delivered*. You reread what you wrote. You try to remember the last time they responded this slowly and what it meant. You draft a follow-up and delete it. You put the phone down. You pick it back up.

Or maybe you're the other version: messages going out constantly, the thread never quiet. You're so heavy in the conversation that the other person barely has room to breathe, yet you're only half in the actual room you're standing in.

Either way, what you're managing isn't the relationship. It's the uncertainty inside you, which, ideally, the relationship is supposed to soothe. You probably learned early that connection wasn't guaranteed, that people went quiet without warning, or that staying close meant staying vigilant. Texting isn't connection; it's a signal. And you're listening for the signal more than you're talking to anyone.

This one runs deep. If this is you, here's what tends to help.

Start with phone-down windows during meals, walks, or time with other people. Practice "send and release"—once it's sent, wait at least thirty minutes before checking for a response. Slow down enough to notice the difference between texting from genuine desire and texting from anxiety. The impulse feels different if you catch it early enough.

Ask yourself honestly: *If I don't hear back for two hours, will I be okay?* If the answer is no, that's not a texting problem. That's the thing worth sitting with.

A PERFORMER: SOMEONE WHO REGULATES THROUGH POSTING

"Being seen helps me feel real."

You post it fast: the win, the milestone, the thing you worked for. Then something shifts. You check who saw it. Who didn't. You notice who liked it and who went quiet. You start to read into that, and, yes, you know you're doing it, and you do it anyway.

The posting isn't the problem. The need underneath it is worth understanding. For a lot of people, this started when love and performance got tangled early, when being impressive was more reliable than just being. Visibility became a way of confirming you existed, that what you did mattered, that you "earned your keep," and that you were enough.

Being seen online isn't the same as being known. And privacy isn't the same as failure.

If this is you, here's what tends to help.

Draft the post, wait a full day, then decide if you still want to share it. You'll know almost immediately whether it was urgent or just anxious. Turn off like and view counts—if the platform allows—removing the feedback loop where you can. Keep a private record of wins that never get posted—just for you, just because they happened.

And before you share anything, ask yourself one question: *Who am I doing this for right now?* The answer will tell you everything.

A CLARIFIER: SOMEONE WHO REGULATES THROUGH RESEARCH AND AI

"If I can make sense of this, I'll feel better."

You use AI to think out loud. To organize options, rehearse a hard conversation, figure out what you want to say. Sometimes it's purely practical. But sometimes it's something that feels too raw or complicated to say to an actual person. So you bring it to AI first, where there's no reaction, no judgment, no risk of being seen in a way you can't take back.

You feel better after. But not always clearer.

That gap is worth paying attention to. AI gives you structure, and when your mind is overloaded, structure feels like relief. But relief and resolution aren't the same thing. You can process something into perfect clarity and still be exactly where you started, because some things don't need better framing. They need to be said.

Some things feel too raw to say out loud to another person.

Those are exactly the things worth saying.

If this is you, here's what tends to help.

Before opening AI or searching anything, spend two minutes writing your own answer first. You know more than you think. Use AI for what it's good at—strategy, logistics, repetitive tasks—and practice bringing the emotional weight to a real person, even just once a week. Notice when research is delaying action rather than informing it, because more information isn't always the answer.

And when you feel the pull to open a tab or start a prompt, ask yourself one question first: *Is this a thinking problem or a feeling problem?*

THE RECLAIM TRUTH

The reaching isn't random. It developed for a reason. The work isn't stopping the behavior; it's graduating it into something more conscious. When you can name what a digital habit is giving you, it stops running the show.

Instead of, "Why can't I stop checking?" ask, "What am I trying to regulate right now?"

That's emotional literacy. And it's where the power lives. Here's what that looked like for me.

There was a season when my life felt like it was coming apart faster than I could process. Outwardly, I may have looked fine, but inside I was in freefall. Like I was suspended somewhere between who I'd been and whoever I was supposed to become next. So I picked up my phone. Not because I decided to. Because it was there. And because the alternative was sitting alone inside that feeling.

What I found wasn't empty. It was steady. Smiling faces talking directly into the camera. Dance trends my body already knew how to follow. Trending audio my brain recognized before it even registered. Questions and answers looping in a rhythm I could track without effort.

Scroll. Something appears. Scroll again. Something else.

No silence. No waiting. No uncertainty. In a moment where nothing in my life felt stable, the feed was. I wasn't just distracting myself. I was regulating. Of course I didn't want to put it down. Because putting it down meant going back into the freefall.

That's the part we don't talk about. Distraction isn't always avoidance. Sometimes it's the closest thing we have to safety in a moment we don't know how to hold.

But safety and solution are not the same thing. The scroll was helping me get through. It just wasn't helping me move forward. Once I could see that, something shifted, enough to start asking a different question: *What do I need right now? What is this doing for me?* That's where the power is. Because once you can name the need, the behavior stops being a mystery. And when it's not a mystery, it's not in control anymore.

While writing this book, one rule I picked up has stayed with me ever since. My editor mentioned it almost in passing. She'd heard it from a friend:

Spend more time with history than prediction.

It landed immediately. I'm a lover of history. Always have been. And the moment she said it, I understood why history calms me in a way the news never does. Prediction content is designed to keep you coming back. The answer is always just out of reach. The next development is always imminent. The loop never closes, because a closed loop has no reason to refresh.

History closes the loop. It hands you something complete. A context. A pattern. A reason. It doesn't ask you to stay anxious for the next update, because the story already happened and you can hold all of it at once.

Perspective is the thing the algorithm is most afraid of giving you.

That rule traveled from a friend to my editor to me to you.

Spend more time with history than prediction.

Pass it on.

YOUR DISTRACTION DIAL

Before you try to change anything, notice what's running.

Red: The loop is deciding for you.

You reach without thinking, scroll without choosing, and check without knowing why. Distraction isn't something you're doing—it's something that's happening to you. You feel drained but can't quite say what the day went to.

Yellow: You can feel the pull.

You catch yourself mid-scroll sometimes. You know your triggers, but you still follow them when you're tired, overwhelmed, or just trying to take the edge off. The awareness is there. The interruption isn't consistent yet.

When you feel the pull, try one question before you open the app: *What am I here for?* Not as a test. Just as a pause. If there's no clear answer, close it. That moment between the impulse and the action is the shift.

Green: You're using it on purpose.

You still reach for distraction, but you know why. You can name what you're regulating. You give yourself the relief when you need it, and you come back when you're ready.

Distraction becomes a tool, not a default.

Ask yourself: Which color describes how distraction has been showing up in your life lately?

Not your worst day. Not your best. Just your pattern.

You don't need to eliminate it. You just need to see it clearly enough to choose it—instead of letting it choose you.

CONNECTION

DISCONNECT TO RECONNECT

As soon as I turned down the gravel road, the weight of the world lifted as I crossed into my own real-life Narnia. Except this wasn't some figment of my imagination. It was two hours north, deep in old-growth redwood forest along the Eel River. A place so special that even money couldn't guarantee admission.

Honk at the second bend in the road, and you'll be met on the flat by a World War II-era bomber truck ready to take you over the river and through the creek to my "happy place": a little stone cabin, built by a family who made their fortune tending to broken-down cars waiting for the ferry to take them from Marin County back to San Francisco before the Golden Gate Bridge. A deep history all but forgotten, yet still alive in the smiling faces that line the cabin's wall of photos—a callback to a different time, when salt-of-the-earth people spent their days building by hand.

The smell of Neutrogena Rainbath drifted from the outdoor shower, while coolers of beer and White Claws lined the walkway. The biggest risk wasn't the current. It was the steep path down to the water, where one wrong step could send you flying. That, or Uncle Scott's infamous bomber truck ride called "the roller coaster," with the kind of drop that steals your stomach, your mind, and every worry you brought with you, giving it back in laughter. Pitch black, terrifying, and somehow exactly what I needed.

As a workaholic techie, this was the moment I looked forward to every year, counting down the days like a child at Christmas. A week or two of sharing one bathroom with fifteen people might sound like a nightmare to most, but it was what we lived for. A place so special that there were more dogs than humans, so secluded that Wi-Fi wasn't even a thought in our minds. Where laughter and conversation were the norm, where families and friends connected over board games at night after spending our days sitting in the river—fully connected and fully together. This is what being present used to feel like: a sense of belonging, simplicity, and aliveness. We didn't plan to disconnect. We just *did*.

Then came the moment that changed everything. Tracy, a mom of five hoping to secure college registration for her son, sang out with victory, "We've got service!" For a second, her joy felt contagious, then it hit me: the grief carried in that faint buzz of digital connection.

The first-gen hotspot blinked to life, its blue light stuttering like it wasn't sure it could hold the signal. In truth, it couldn't. It ran hot, a modern campfire where we huddled around our devices for hollow warmth. Even though I didn't open my phone, something switched on inside me, a doorway back to deadlines, noise, the pressure to always be "on." The bend in the river stayed the same, but we didn't. The silence that had felt sacred now felt awkward.

The water still shimmered, the redwoods stood strong, but our attention had already drifted downstream.

The river didn't change that year. We did.

Sometimes I still think about that bend in the river, and how part of me is always trying to find my way back there. Not to disconnect forever. Just to remember what it felt like when presence was the default and not the decision. Every year, as soon as I cross that invisible line onto the gravel road and unload, I put my phone in my backpack under my bunk in the sleeping cabin. *Off*, because I choose off.

That's the difference I didn't understand then. It was never about being unreachable. It was about making the choice. The hotspot didn't take anything from us that night. It just made visible something that had already changed—the fact that being present had stopped being our default and started being something we had to decide.

Now I decide. Every year. On the same gravel road, at the same bend in the river.

SOCIAL MEDIA MAKEOVER

We didn't lose our need for connection. We lost control of where we look for it.

The best piece of advice I ever received from an influencer was to unfollow anyone who made me feel sad or less than. Anyone who made me shrink instead of expanding my life. Your feed should reflect who you're becoming, not who you fear you'll never be.

That meant letting go of the accounts that kept me stuck in a version of my life I had outgrown—the high school friends I didn't talk to anymore and the food bloggers who made me wish I'd started my blog sooner. Which brought me back to the reason I hadn't.

My stepfather told me once, "You can't sell blue sky." He didn't understand how any of it worked—how something intangible could become income, or how content could become a career—so he dismissed it. I will never forget. Not because it hurt, though it did. But because deep down, I knew this was the future and I'd be missing out if I didn't do it.

I'd be lying if I said I didn't believe him at first. Watching those same women succeed felt like proof I'd missed my chance, like their timelines were moving forward and mine had already stalled. But they weren't ahead of me. I was just measuring my life against a rule that was never true.

I named my company Blue Sky Rituals LLC. Most people don't know why. That's the point. It's my quiet reminder to do what calls me, to keep going when others don't believe in the dream, to not worry about whether the payoff makes sense to anyone else.

He was wrong. You can sell blue sky. And it's very real.

For a long time, I carried his criticism like a weight I didn't know I was holding. The stepfather who fixed engines didn't understand how you could build something from nothing but an idea and a domain name. But the thing about being told you can't is that often it has a way of becoming the very reason you do. Not out of spite. Out of something quieter. The need to find out for yourself what's possible.

It's the same voice that feeds imposter syndrome, the one that insists you're not talented enough, disciplined enough, or special enough to succeed. Unfollowing them wasn't a sign of envy or pettiness. It was choosing to step out of an ever-tightening, restrictive story into one where my own voice had room to breathe. It was the moment I started rewriting my story.

Clearing your feed is about making room for a better world. Because when you remove what drains you, you finally create space for the content, voices, and ideas that expand you. Social media can be a mentor, a lifeline, a spark. But only when you choose what you're feeding on.

Here is the part most people forget: No one else knows your digital life, what your feed looks like, or how it makes you feel. We all walk around with private ecosystems of content that shape us in ways most people never see.

Sometimes the things we consume online entertain us, while others quietly influence how we see ourselves. Maybe the feed leaves you feeling a little behind, a little not-enough, or like everyone else is somehow getting life right while you're still figuring it out. It happens to all of us.

Even people who don't consider themselves influencers now treat their accounts like picture-perfect personal ads, sharing the brightest, most successful version of their lives. Somewhere along the way, social media quietly shifted from a place to connect into a place to perform. We don't just post anymore; we curate. We edit. We stage. We manage perception.

What once felt like casual sharing now comes with an unspoken pressure to look happy, accomplished, attractive, busy, and fulfilled—sometimes all at once. Vacations become content. Milestones become proof. Even ordinary moments are filtered through the question: *How will this look?*

And because everyone is involved, it's easy to forget that what we're comparing ourselves to isn't a full life—it's a highlight reel. A carefully selected slice of reality designed to communicate success, ease, and momentum. Even when the truth behind the screen is far more complicated.

Most of the heaviness we feel online doesn't come from envy alone. It comes from assumptions we don't even realize we're making. We assume other people are happier than they are. More confident than they feel. More certain. We mistake presentation for truth and visibility for validation.

Influencers simply make this dynamic more explicit. They are paid to present a certain image because that *is* the business model. They sell a dream of effortlessness, beauty, freedom, abundance because dreams convert better than reality. The polished homes, the flawless routines, the "this changed my life" captions aren't meant to reflect the whole picture. They're meant to drive desire.

It's no more real than a Hollywood set. The lighting is intentional. The angles are chosen. The mess is cropped out. And that discount code? It exists to drive revenue, not to save you money.

But the subtler impact comes from watching people who *aren't* influencers adopt the same language, aesthetics, and rhythms. When friends, coworkers, and acquaintances start presenting their lives as brands in progress, comparison becomes constant and inescapable. You're no longer just measuring yourself against celebrities or creators—you're measuring yourself against everyone.

For a long time, I didn't see this. I thought everyone else was simply doing life better than me. I internalized the gap between what I felt and what I saw, assuming it meant I was behind.

I even went into debt trying to fix that feeling. It started small—Primal Kitchen Protein Powder, Trader Joe's cauliflower gnocchi, the kind of recipes that came with a lifestyle attached. Cooking influencers who were really lifestyle influencers in disguise. Then it was home items and high-end vacuums. Which led to luxury vacations. Each purchase felt like a step closer to the life I was watching on my screen, the white-house aesthetic—part minimalist with a collection of houseplants and a dash of granola energy.

I didn't realize what was happening until I looked around at everything I'd bought. My credit card statements were proof that I had spent my way through someone else's highlight reel. Google Photos albums full of moments I'd curated rather than lived. A life that looked right from the outside and felt hollow from the inside.

I hadn't been shopping. I'd been auditioning for a version of myself that was never mine to begin with.

It didn't work. It never does.

I tell you this not to shame the impulse— I understand it completely—but I think most people are doing some version of the same thing without realizing it. The feed doesn't just show you what's possible. It quietly suggests what you're lacking. And the gap between what you see and what you have is exactly where the spending, the shrinking, and the comparing live.

But realizing that none of this is personal—that it's the architecture of the system, not a reflection of your worth—frees something inside you. You stop blaming yourself, you stop feeling behind, and you start seeing the feed for what it is, which allows you to decide what you want to believe about yourself.

Your feed is a compass that points toward the life you're creating, whether you realize it or not.

Once you stop consuming on autopilot, social media stops being a comparison trap and becomes a teacher. It becomes the mentor you didn't know you needed, the encouragement you never had, and the spark that leads you somewhere new. Used intentionally, it can guide you, grow you, and remind you of what's possible.

Curate your feed with purpose. Add one account that makes you think bigger and remove one that makes you feel smaller. Notice how quickly your inner world shifts in response to changes in your digital life.

I felt this shift most acutely on a day when the bridesmaids' thread had been going for six hours straight—every notification a new opinion, a new task, a new version of myself I was supposed to show up as for someone else's perfect day.

I was scrolling aimlessly until I landed on creator Kat Stickler's video. You may know the ones—her "friend that" series, where she does impressions of either someone like you, or someone you know, with an accuracy that makes you both laugh and wince. There's the friend who never speaks up for herself. The friend who argues every point. Kat delivers it all with a vivacious smile you genuinely cannot look away from, the kind that makes you feel like she's performing just for you. And she does it in under sixty seconds.

That one post didn't just entertain me. It gave me the permission I didn't know I needed to simply step into who I am. That is the part people miss when they dismiss influencers. They see the gloss and miss the humanity. These creators poured pieces of themselves into their content, and those pieces found the parts of me that needed encouragement, clarity, and comfort. They are strangers, but somehow they have been companions in my growth. They have been teachers without knowing they were teaching, and mirrors I did not expect to look into.

So the next time you're scrolling through your feed, pause for a moment and ask yourself: *Is this content shrinking me or supporting me?*

Each week, add one account that expands you. Remove one that quietly drains you. No justification. No list. No metrics.

UNFILTERED YOU

There's a moment on the internet that still stops me every time. It's when someone posts a video with no smoothing filter, no contouring sparkles, no face-shaping magic: just their real skin, real pores, and real expressions.

At first it's jarring. Then grounding. Because underneath all the edits and algorithms, that's what we're craving most: a return to something real. It's not about being perfect, aesthetic, or even brave. It's about being awake to the fact that your digital environment is shaping you just as much as you're shaping it.

This is what influencer and comedian Elyse Myers does so beautifully. She doesn't sell the perfect life. She shares the human one: showing up despite awkwardness and anxiety, with humor and honesty that cuts through a world of heavily edited content. She reminds us that authenticity isn't a strategy.

But here's what most people don't realize: It's also not neutral.

Every unfiltered video, every honest caption, every time someone shows up as themselves instead of their highlight reel—that's not just brave. That's a signal. And the algorithm is reading it. Researchers are finding that users who engage deliberately, who seek out different voices and interact with content that breaks the pattern, actively change how the algorithm learns. Passive scrolling feeds the loop. Intentional engagement rewires it.

Elyse isn't just being authentic. She's training her algorithm—and yours—toward something more human.

Here's the truth most people skip: Your digital environment is also your psychological environment, and curating your feed is another way of creating your identity.

If you follow chaos, you feel chaotic. If you follow comparison, you feel behind. If you follow inspiration, you start imagining different possibilities for your own life. If you follow honesty, you find permission to be honest.

Social media isn't neutral—it's a mirror. But *you* get to choose what stays in the reflection. Most people get stuck here, and the pushback I hear is always the same: "I can't change my algorithm." But the truth is every click is a vote. That might sound like motivational fluff, until you look at what researchers are finding.

In a 2025 study published in *MIS Quarterly*, researchers Marta Stelmaszak, Mareike Möhlmann, and Carsten Sørensen found that algorithmic systems depend on human behavior to function and improve. Studying Uber, they showed that people constantly teach the system through both passive and active signals. Some information is gathered automatically as a byproduct of using the app, such as location and movement data. Other signals come from the choices users make, such as accepting requests or altering routes. Together, these actions shape how the algorithm learns and adapts over time.

This connects to something psychologists have understood about the brain for decades. A 2021 study in *Nature Communications* by Björn Lindström and colleagues analyzed more than a million social media posts through the lens of computational reinforcement learning. They found that our online behavior follows the same reward-based loops that shape habits more broadly: We adjust our engagement to maximize social rewards, and what gets reinforced gets repeated.

As the ride-sharing research demonstrated—and Lindström's findings on social media reinforce—the platform isn't simply influencing your behavior from the outside. It is continuously learning from it, adapting to the signals you provide and becoming increasingly effective at capturing your attention.

Your algorithm isn't some all-knowing entity that has you locked in. The algorithm behaves like a student, constantly learning from the signals you provide. So, no, you're not erasing fifteen years of data in a weekend detox. But you are influencing what your mind is repeatedly fed.

You train your algorithm the same way you train your nervous system: through awareness, repetition, and intention.

THE GIFT OF PRESENCE

In *The Five Love Languages: How to Express Heartfelt Commitment to Your Mate,* author Gary Chapman presents five love languages—words, touch, time, service, and gifts. His framework got me thinking about what makes each of those expressions meaningful in the first place. I would argue that beneath them all is something even more fundamental: presence. Not a sixth love language, but the foundation that allows the other five to be felt. Without it, even our most thoughtful gestures can ring hollow.

Presence is attention made visible, and it is the most profound form of love. We've mistaken constant connection for closeness, but it's attention that builds intimacy.

There was a night I put my phone down after scrolling and tried to remember what I had just seen. Not in a deep, reflective way. Just casually, like you do when something's supposed to stick. Nothing came up. Not one post. Not one idea. Not even a vague impression. I'd watched somewhere between twenty and thirty videos—fifteen, maybe twenty seconds each—and my brain was just fried. Like it had processed so much, it had retained nothing. And when Sean asked what I was watching, I paused. "Just videos," I said. Because that was all I had. Not a title, not a topic, not even a feeling. Just videos.

That's when something subtle but important shifted. It wasn't just that I had lost time. It was that I had traded something real for something that didn't even register. It didn't feel like I had chosen to spend my time that way. It felt like something had quietly spent it *for* me.

I wrote about this years ago in *Be Present*, but it's even truer now. Being fully present in the moment is the most radical act in a world that is increasingly distracted.

True presence reshapes the brain.

When we meet someone's eyes, mirror neurons activate, the circuits that help us feel what others feel. That's how empathy and attunement grow, moment by moment. Divided attention does the opposite. It reduces trust and weakens connection. So while presence builds empathy, divided attention erodes it.

"Unplugging is not a break from real life—it's a return to it."
—Tiffany Shlain, *24/6: The Power of Unplugging One Day a Week*

We live in the age of algorithmic intimacy, where our devices study us more closely than some of the people we love. AI learns our rhythms—when we're lonely, when we can't sleep, when we're most likely to reach for distraction instead of depth.

If you tracked the videos my feed showed me each day, it would look like one of those temperature blankets where someone knits the year's weather into rows of colored yarn. Except mine would map my emotional weather: Sad days brought dancing videos and motivational quotes, hopeful days brought manifestation and tarot cards, burnout days brought corporate parodies. No yarn required, just videos I'll never remember watching. But together they'd show you a map of my life, one the algorithm drew more accurately than I could.

These systems don't just compete for attention; they anticipate it. They fill every quiet space before stillness has a chance to arrive. I often grab my phone when I'm bored, picking it up and wondering what I should even do with it. Sometimes I put it back down because I know I'm using it for comfort. Other times

I give in and let the algorithm take me where it wants to keep me—logged on and silent. Either way, I never seem satisfied. Not when I say no, and not when I give in. I feel lost and pulled, yet guilty nonetheless.

The problem was worst in the mornings. I'd lose an hour to who knows what, then be left feeling drained before I'd even started my day. So I moved my charger to my desk on the other side of the house. Immediately, I felt naked. As a woman who lives alone, the thought spiraled: What if I needed it? My phone had become this force field that would protect me from anything. I thought about fires and earthquakes and, yes, even tsunamis. Once I acknowledged how ridiculous that sounded, I made the change permanent. Because truly, my phone is a bigger risk than all those combined.

The algorithm had learned to fill every gap. And I'd learned to let it.

But presence, actual human presence, can't be optimized. It only exists in the gaps the algorithm hasn't yet learned to fill.

A friend from high school was always on her phone. I'd drive up to see her and, as soon as I walked in, she'd be on the couch scrolling, half-listening. I came for companionship and only got a word here or there. I thought it was me, until she had her first child and it was the same thing. That made me feel okay for a moment, until I realized he wasn't getting the attention he needed either.

I didn't want to become that. But I was already halfway there—just with a different screen.

I'm a planner, and I love strategizing with ChatGPT. The app lets me dream bigger without judgment. It's genuinely useful. But I'd started outsourcing my thoughts. I'd break from conversations for a sideline huddle with my bot, as if the algorithm's validation mattered more than theirs. Until Sean called me out.

"I wish you'd asked for my opinion," he said.

That really hit me. I was outsourcing my connection. The algorithm couldn't replace him. But I'd been acting like it could. So now we do phones-down time. We stand in the kitchen and talk about our goals and desires. It's a way of reclaiming our commitment to each other in a part of the house that is not completely absorbed by technology. A return to something older, when kitchens were the heartbeat of the home.

Here's what it looks like when someone gets it right.

I had a director once who kept her phone on the conference table during every meeting, but for our one-on-ones, she left it at her desk. No buzz. No glance. No competition with whatever might light up and pull the room in a different direction.

Something about knowing the phone wasn't there changed the texture of the whole conversation. There was no divided attention to account for. No wondering if I was about to lose her mid-sentence. It was just the two of us in the room for forty-five minutes, and that was the whole point.

I felt it immediately. Not as a policy. As a choice she made every single time. She never announced it. Never made it a thing. She just showed up without it. And because of that, I showed up differently too. More honest. More direct. More willing to say the thing I'd been sitting on.

Presence, it turns out, is contagious.

But that kind of presence takes practice. Because the moment we find stillness, the noise comes looking for us again. The modern world doesn't like silence. It wants every pause filled, every moment accounted for. Autoplay, infinite scroll, and push notifications are anti-presence technologies designed to harvest attention. When you log off, you disrupt the system that profits from distraction.

What part of your humanity thrives when the algorithm is quiet?

You might not know yet. That's the point.

You've been interrupted so long, you've forgotten what your unmediated thoughts sound like. I know, because I asked myself the same question. What am I most afraid of in that silence? My inability to care for myself, to trust myself, to be productive and liked.

Yet that's where reconnection begins. Being bored feels like watching paint dry. You're left alone with yourself. And if you get to the part where you're not making mental lists or planning your next move, it can feel vast, like you're collapsing into yourself at the same time. On the other side of that collapse is something real.

Presence doesn't require grand gestures, just small, sacred pauses. The ones that fit between sips of coffee, or moments of eye contact across a kitchen table.

Presence isn't something you schedule. It's something you surrender to, because you can't automate empathy. You have to arrive for it.

When you give your full attention, you give your love fully.

YOUR CONNECTION DIAL

Before you move into the next section, take a moment to notice where you are.

Red: You're physically present, but mentally somewhere else. Half listening, half scrolling, one foot already out the door. The people around you can feel it even if they don't say it. Connection is happening around you, not with you.

Yellow: You're mostly there. You put the phone down but you're still thinking about it. You're engaged, but distracted in ways you can feel underneath. The conversation is real, but something is slightly muted.

Green: You're in the room fully. Your attention is placed on purpose and the people around you can feel the difference. This is where trust gets built, where people tell you the tender things, where connection happens.

Ask yourself honestly: Which color describes how you've been showing up in your closest relationships lately?

You don't have to fix it right now. Just name it. Because you can't choose differently until you can see clearly where you are.

HEARTS IN THE ROOM

This is the real cost of distraction—not lost productivity, but the slow erosion of trust, the way people stop offering the tender parts of themselves once they learn you're not really there to listen.

Relationships rarely rupture dramatically anymore. Rather, they dissolve quietly, through a hundred tiny moments where no one stays. The glance at the phone mid-sentence. The half-answer while scrolling. The dinner where everyone is technically present and nobody actually arrives. Each one small enough to forgive. Together, enough to create distance that neither person can quite name.

Presence is leadership. Not the résumé kind. The human kind. The kind that changes the atmosphere of a room.

Last weekend, I sat across from a friend I hadn't seen in months. We were catching up over tacos, the kind of meal where the chips keep coming and the conversation feels easy—where you think you're present, but you're actually just waiting for your turn to talk. Then I felt it, that phantom itch, the whisper: *"What if someone needs you?"*

My hand moved toward my pocket before I even decided to check. But this time, I caught myself. Nothing needed me. So I let the urge pass. I put both hands back on the table and chose to land in the moment. And in that small, ordinary act, something opened.

My friend then told me about the panic attack she had last month in a grocery-store parking lot, how she'd sat in her car for twenty minutes before she could go inside. Her voice dropped as she said it, like she was testing whether the room was safe enough to hold something fragile.

That's the quiet magic of presence. When you root yourself in the moment, others soften. When you listen, they tell you who they are, and when you show up—fully engaged, without one foot already out the door—they find the courage too.

People don't remember your every post. They remember your eyes on them. They remember being chosen.

At your next meal, put your phone out of reach. Not face down, not "just in case." *Away.* See what returns to the room when you do. Who's been waiting for you to show up?

Presence isn't a skill you master once. It's a choice you make, meal after meal, conversation after conversation. And every time you choose it, you're not just showing up—you're building trust.

Ways to Choose Again... *So your habits don't run on autopilot.*

Most habits don't feel like decisions. They feel like momentum. You reach, scroll, click, switch—without ever noticing the moment you could have done something else.

Choosing again doesn't mean getting it right the first time. It means catching it mid-pattern. Pausing just long enough to see it. And deciding, even once, to go *intentionally* in a different direction.

That's how patterns change.

WALKING BACK TO YOURSELF

I met Jessica DeAngelo through my speaker mastermind. She's the founder of Hike to Become, a strategic advisory firm that takes leadership teams out of the boardroom and onto the trail. Her method blends neuroscience, nature immersion, and business strategy to unlock the kind of thinking that rarely happens behind a screen. Her argument is simple: Your best ideas aren't stuck. They're just trapped in the wrong environment.

After doing one of her guided sessions, I decided to join her Hike to Become Challenge. The challenge has four parts, which Jessica built into the name itself.

H is for hike or walk: no mountain required. A purposeful walk counts.

I is for in nature: outside, fully immersed.

K is for keep tech off: phone away, headphones out, no podcasts, no music, no emails. Just your thoughts, which turns out to be the hardest part.

E is for every day: thirty-one consecutive days. That's how long it takes for the habit to stop feeling like effort and start feeling like you.

I'll be honest—the first time I considered leaving my phone behind, even for a walk, something in me resisted. Hard. There's a name for it: nomophobia, the anxiety and panic that comes from being separated from your smartphone. I felt it. Walking my dog alone without my phone felt irresponsible. What if there was an emergency? What if something happened, and I had no way to reach anyone? The fear was real even when the threat wasn't.

But I tried it anyway. Thirty minutes a day, no phone, no podcast, no distractions.

I noticed things I'd stopped seeing. The way the amber light broke through the leaves. A stranger who smiled without needing anything back. The quiet that arrived about ten minutes in, when my nervous system finally understood—and believed—I wasn't missing anything.

Connection doesn't require a signal. It requires presence.

Try it once. Leave the phone behind. Walk somewhere without documentation.

Notice what shows up when you stop reaching for proof that you were there.

GROWTH

CREATOR, NOT COMMODITY

Type "dress" into Nordstrom. Four hundred sixty pages appear. You scroll. You filter. You open five tabs for dresses that all look exactly the same.

Amazon is as endless as the river it was named after. Different brands, same dress. Different name, same factory. You read reviews from people you don't know about a product no one needed this many versions of. You came for a dress. You leave an hour later with nothing. Slightly irritated. Weirdly tired. Like you did something, but didn't actually move.

That feeling has a name. The Danish philosopher Søren Kierkegaard saw it coming long before the internet existed. Anxiety doesn't come from having too few choices. It comes from having too many. Endless possibility, he argued, doesn't liberate the self—it overwhelms it. When every path feels open, nothing feels solid. What looks like freedom becomes paralysis.

Social media makes this collapse visible. It doesn't just show you who you could become. It shows you every version simultaneously. Every physique, every morning routine, every career trajectory, every correct way to live. The issue isn't a lack of inspiration—it's the avalanche of it, which causes the nervous system to lock down so you don't expand. You don't feel empowered. You feel perpetually behind. Growth doesn't stall from lack of motivation. It stalls from too many mirrors and no compass.

The truth was simpler and scarier: I wasn't looking for motivation. I was looking for permission. Permission to exist in a body I had spent years trying to outrun. Then something changed.

I stumbled on a post by former international model turned transformational coach Nikki Sharp. It was 2018, and she was promoting her cookbook *Meal Prep Your Way to Weight Loss: 28 Days to a Fitter, Healthier You.* Her *Adulting* podcast became my secret ritual. I would come home from work exhausted, sink into my claw-foot bathtub, and listen to her and her cohost, Zack Peter, as they interviewed guests who discussed everything from wellness to self-discovery. It was my treat after a long day. More than that, though, it was a lifeline.

Over time, I watched her change—not in the way she ate, but in the way she thought and the way she talked about *purpose* rather than the pursuit of perfection. Her mindset shifted, and something inside me responded to that. It was like seeing a door open in her world, and realizing it was a door I could walk through too.

What changed me was watching *her* change. She didn't feel like an influencer but more like a friend, pulling me toward a version of myself I hadn't met yet.

Through her, I discovered motivational speaker Tony Robbins, who hosted the co-founders of BossBabe—Natalie Ellis and Danielle Canty—alongside authors Lewis Howes and Trent Shelton and entrepreneur Dean Graziosi in the many free webinars I attended. I remember watching them and thinking, *I want to do that.*

I joined The Société by BossBabe, where I was introduced to high performance coach Brendon Burchard—and the idea that changed everything for me wasn't about hustle. It was about alignment. How your daily actions either close the gap between who you are and who you're becoming, or quietly widen it.

From there, it became a waterfall. Marketing expert Jenna Kutcher showed me how Pinterest could become a platform. Spiritual teacher Gabby Bernstein opened a door I hadn't known existed—manifestation, intention, the idea that what you focus on grows. And author Mel Robbins gave me something I hadn't expected: proof that a simple framework, delivered with conviction, could change the trajectory of someone's life. One account led to another, and suddenly my feed wasn't making me smaller. It was expanding me. For the first time, I felt like I'd found where I fit.

My digital life wasn't about aesthetics anymore. It was about possibilities.

Their content didn't trigger my insecurities—it awakened my ambition. It reminded me that I wanted to write, speak, teach, and help people. It showed me there was a version of my life I hadn't allowed myself to imagine yet.

That's when I realized social media isn't inherently the problem. It reflects what you're reaching for. But even that wasn't the full picture. Because what I was consuming only mattered once my attention could stay with something long enough to let it change me.

Growth wasn't coming from the feed. It was coming from what my mind was able to do with it.

When I was seeking control, my feed mirrored that. But when I was ready for growth, my feed became the classroom where I found my calling. And looking back now, I realize something wild: None of this was random. Every one of those people was connected. They'd spoken on each other's podcasts, shared stages, swapped interviews, recommended the same books, and lived in overlapping circles online.

It was like stepping into a hidden mentorship map I didn't know existed. One person led me to the next, not by accident, but because I was finally ready for the kind of life they were teaching. Social media wasn't pulling me away from myself anymore; it was guiding me toward the person I was becoming.

That's what a curated feed can do when you're finally ready. It doesn't just show you what's possible.

It shows you who you already are.

I began to see the work differently too. Tony Robbins and Dean Graziosi built their entire businesses around one idea: Serve the you of five years ago. They taught me that "selling is simply service in motion" and that the most meaningful work comes from turning your lived experience into something that helps someone else rise.

I saw how much intention and heart went into consistently showing up as a creator. I saw the deadlines behind brand deals, the endless ideation of what to post and when, and the emotional labor of letting people into your real life—even when they criticize the very vulnerability you offered them.

Every piece of content stopped feeling like a performance and started feeling like what it truly is: a small act of service. A love letter to the people on the other side of the screen. A reminder that someone is trying every day to make this world more understandable, more beautiful, or, at least, a little easier to get through.

It's easy to judge influencers from a distance. It is harder to acknowledge the truth: Our feeds reflect the people we choose to learn from, laugh with, and let into our inner worlds. We are not passive consumers. We are curators of our digital environment, and these influencers became part of mine, because their work made me feel seen.

And that realization changed something fundamental. I didn't just want to consume anymore. I wanted to create.

GROWTH THEATER

This is the part that took me longer to admit. I am a chronic consumer of growth content. Podcasts on the commute. Books on the nightstand. Courses I sign up for and never finish. Apparently, my hobby is buying courses. For years, I told myself this was learning. An investment in my future. But eventually I had to face it: I wasn't growing. I was *performing* growth. Consuming improvement instead of practicing it.

I call it growth theater. And it's everywhere.

Students watch videos about productivity instead of doing the assignments. They listen to podcasts about focus instead of sitting down and focusing. They consume content about the life they want to build while avoiding the discomfort of building it.

It makes sense. Growth content feels like progress because the brain doesn't easily distinguish between learning something and doing it. But real growth has a different texture. It's slower. More focused. Slightly uncomfortable. It requires staying with something long enough for it to change you.

That's what we keep trading away.

The practice I started offering myself—and eventually my students—is almost embarrassingly simple: *For every one thing you consume, apply one thing you learned before you consume more.*

That's it. Just one. Before you open the next tab. That shift moves growth from accumulation to integration. You stop feeling behind. You start feeling capable.

I learned this the hard way early in my career—a last-minute off-site in San Francisco, in a room I wasn't sure I belonged in.

Two months into my first university recruiting role, a leap from higher education to corporate tech that felt like being called up to the big leagues. I was the youngest person there by a meaningful margin, and too nervous to do anything but nod.

The room was floor-to-ceiling glass on two sides. The Bay stretched out below us, the bridges in the distance doing what San Francisco views do—making everything feel enormous and possible. There were five HRBPs and one senior recruiter.

The VP of HR had required some prereading: an excerpt from Carol S. Dweck's *Mindset: The New Psychology of Success.*

But I hadn't gotten it in time. So I sat there with the words on the page, the Bay in the distance, and a room full of people applying growth mindset theory to their actual lives—their careers, their failures, their relationships—laughing and challenging each other and sharing things I didn't expect people to share in a professional setting. Open in a way that felt like permission. Like this was what rooms were supposed to feel like.

I didn't speak. I was too stunned to speak. I just absorbed.

Nobody in that room was performing growth. They were *doing* it. That's the difference I'd been missing.

Something unexpected happened in that stillness. *Permission.* Permission to grow through life rather than just manage it. Permission to show up open and willing, even when you don't have the metrics.

That night, we went to a Brazilian steakhouse. Too much wine. Way too much meat. Successful people at the peak of their careers still going back to one idea from a book because it had cracked something open.

I understood then that growth wasn't a productivity strategy. It was a way of moving through the world. And once you see it, you cannot unsee it. You meet someone, and within minutes you can feel it—the way they talk about a setback, the way they approach something unfamiliar, the way they hold a mistake. Fixed or open. Defended or curious. It shows up in everything.

I finally had words for what I'd been reaching for all along: the freedom to grow through life, not just manage it.

THINKING ALLOWED

Long before focus became a productivity metric, Maria Montessori understood something more humane. You might know her name from expensive preschools or beautifully crafted wooden toys. Montessori was an Italian physician and educator who spent decades in the early 1900s observing how children learn when given the right conditions.

Concentration was not something to demand from a person, she believed, but something that emerged naturally when the environment stopped pulling them apart. In her classrooms, children were not "corrected" or pressured into focus. They became focused because the space around them allowed their attention to settle. And when it did, something profound happened. The child became more themselves.

Montessori believed concentration was restorative. That when attention stays in one place long enough, it doesn't just complete tasks—it rebuilds the self.

That idea feels almost radical now, because our environments are no longer designed to let attention settle. They are designed to interrupt it. Capture it. Redirect it before anything deeper can take hold.

Cal Newport, author and digital-minimalism advocate, calls the alternative "deep work."

The people who've figured this out aren't more disciplined. They've removed the need to be. They work in conditions where one thing exists at a time. When they're working, they're working. When they're done, they're done.

Focus isn't something they fight for. It's already been decided.

That's the shift. It's not that they're better at resisting distraction. It's that they've removed the need to resist it in the first place.

I saw what this looks like up close, with a student at the University of California, Berkeley. She was capable, ambitious, and deeply motivated. From the outside, nothing looked wrong. But inside she felt scattered. Reading took longer. Writing felt harder. Every study session dissolved into switching between tabs, apps, notifications, anything that offered an easier hit than the work in front of her. She blamed herself for lacking discipline. The truth: She had too many interruptions.

She didn't delete her apps or quit social media. She made one small change—she rearranged her environment, so her attention had somewhere to land. Phone out of reach. One screen. One document. Notifications off during work blocks—not forever, just long enough.

The change came quietly. One afternoon, she noticed she'd been reading for nearly forty minutes without checking her phone. Not because she was forcing herself. Because she forgot it was there. Her body felt different. Less tense. Less braced. When she finished the paragraph, she realized she remembered what she had read. Not just the words. The ideas.

Later, while writing, she reached the end of a page and felt something she hadn't felt in months. *Trust.* She trusted that her mind could still hold something long enough to shape it. That moment mattered more than any productivity gain, because it changed how she saw herself.

She was not broken. Her attention had been fragmented.

As the weeks went on, the changes accumulated. She felt less anxious before starting her work. Decision-making felt easier. Her thinking felt more continuous, less jumpy. She was not doing more. She was staying longer. And staying longer allowed something essential to return—authorship. The sense that her thoughts were hers again, not assembled from fragments of everyone else's.

And this is where the feeling becomes familiar. Because I know this shift. I've lived it.

The first time it happened, I didn't even notice. I looked up from my book and two hours had passed. My coffee had gone cold. My phone was face down on the table. And I felt like I had just woken up from the best kind of sleep.

You know the kind of focus I mean. The Rory Gilmore kind. The kind in which the world goes quiet without disappearing. Where a book is open, coffee is nearby, and time stops asking anything of you. No optimization or urgency. No one watching. Just a mind fully inside a thought, staying long enough for something to take shape.

On *Gilmore Girls,* Rory never looked productive in the modern sense. She was absorbed. Hunched over a library table at Yale or tucked into a corner at Luke's, surrounded by stacks of books and half-finished notebooks, forgetting to check the clock because her attention had gone somewhere deeper. That was the magic. Her focus was not about output. It was about becoming. You could feel it happening in real time. Each page she read, each essay she rewrote, each conversation she stayed present for was quietly shaping who she was. Less through pressure than devotion.

That is what this student touched when her attention finally stayed long enough to rest. It was the kind of concentration that makes you feel like *yourself* again. The kind that reminds you that your mind is not a machine to manage, but a place where you can actually live.

I didn't even know I was grieving this until I felt it return. The ability to sink into something without guilt. Without the nagging sense that I should be doing three other things simultaneously. Without performing my own focus for an invisible audience that does not exist.

For so many of us, Rory represented a version of womanhood where thinking deeply was allowed. Where ambition did not require burnout. Where being inward was not a flaw. Where attention was something you gave because it mattered, not because someone was measuring it. Maybe that is why we loved her so much. She proved that a woman could be ambitious without being available. Smart without being useful. Absorbed in her own mind, without apologizing for it. That's what it looked like to be a creator—before the internet taught us to perform.

And that is what returned in that moment. A sense of self that could finally settle.

This is what Montessori meant. Concentration does not just improve performance. It organizes identity. When attention stays with one thing long enough, the self adheres to it. Confidence grows not from achievement, but from the lived experience of being able to remain present with your own mind.

This is why growth cannot be forced through discipline alone. Discipline without alignment creates compliance. Alignment, meaning your habits matching your goals and your actions matching your values.

This is the difference between being a consumer of attention and a creator of self. When attention is constantly pulled outward, identity becomes reactive. You start your morning scrolling someone else's routine, then spend the rest of the day wondering why yours feels wrong. You shape yourself in response to what you see, what you compare, what you consume. But when attention is allowed to remain, identity becomes generative. You begin creating from within, not performing for what is watching. Growth doesn't require becoming someone new. It requires staying with yourself long enough to recognize who you already are.

Once you see that concentration builds the self, the question shifts. It is no longer: *"How do I focus better?"* It becomes: *"What kind of self is my environment helping me become?"*

That is where choice returns. Not as pressure, as possibility. Not as something you chase, but as something you recognize when your mind finally stops running.

There was a season when I was consuming far more than I was creating. I was listening to podcasts, joining webinars, saving posts, gathering ideas from people I admired. It all looked like growth. But underneath it, I could feel my own voice getting harder to hear.

So I made one small change: Before I opened anything else in the morning, I gave myself a little protected space to think first. Just coffee, a notebook, and whatever was already in me.

At first, the silence felt unnatural. Then it started to feel like relief. My thoughts got clearer. My work got more honest. I stopped mistaking consumption for progress.

What came back wasn't just focus. It was authorship.

YOUR GROWTH DIAL

Montessori called it the "prepared environment." Here's what that looks like for your attention right now.

Red: Your attention is mostly reactive. You are consuming more than you are creating, comparing more than you are choosing, and starting the day in someone else's mental world before you've entered your own. Growth feels noisy, pressured, and strangely hollow.

Yellow: You want depth, and you've had glimpses of it, but your attention still leaks. You protect your focus sometimes, but not consistently. You know what helps, yet you still default to whatever is easiest when you're tired, restless, or overwhelmed.

Green: Your attention has somewhere to land. You are not perfectly focused all the time, but you're relating to growth more intentionally. You protect space for your own thoughts, your own work, and your own becoming. What you consume supports what you are trying to build instead of replacing it.

Ask yourself: Which color describes the environment in which your growth has been happening lately? Which color describes your general day-to-day pattern?

There is no need to force yourself into Green overnight. You just need to see clearly what conditions you're working with now. Growth begins with basic recognition.

Ways Back to Yourself... *So you don't lose yourself in the process.*

It doesn't happen all at once. You don't wake up one day feeling disconnected from who you are. It's quieter than that. You drift. You adapt. You adjust to what's expected, what's easy, what keeps things moving, until something feels slightly off. You're just not fully ... well, you.

Coming back involves catching that moment before you dismiss it or explain it away. Catch the thought you almost didn't say, the choice you almost didn't make. Such small things add up.

This will help keep you from leaving in the first place.

IMPACT

FAILED INFLUENCER

I used to humorously call myself a "failed influencer." It was easier than explaining why I had 13,000 LinkedIn followers but rarely posted. Easier than defending why I'd built a following through years of recruiting at major tech companies like Uber, Google, Visa, then went quiet the moment I tried to say something that mattered to *me*, not just my employer. The joke was a shield, letting me own the narrative before someone else could use it against me.

But I wasn't a failed influencer. I was an in-person influencer. I just didn't have language for it yet.

Coaches told me I couldn't make the impact I wanted without posting online. One told me I'd never serve millions if I didn't show up consistently on social media. Another said to document my book-writing journey—take people along, build community through transparency. What they called bravery felt, in my body, like exposure without consent. Performing this work of creating something profound felt ironic at best, disingenuous at worst.

I decided not to continue with these coaches. I wasn't going to perform my way through writing a book about reclaiming yourself. If I couldn't practice what I was preaching, what was I even writing?

Then came SXSW EDU. I'd submitted a proposal: "*Reclaim Focus: How Students Can Thrive in the Attention Economy.*" To secure one of the coveted speaking spots, I needed votes. Hundreds of them.

The strategy everyone recommended? To activate my LinkedIn. When I told a faculty member I wasn't doing that, she scoffed. "*Good luck with that.*" The thing is: Many of those people followed me because they wanted jobs at the companies I recruited for. They didn't know me. They knew my access. So I made a different choice.

I went back to Sonoma State, my campus. The place where my mom worked in the math department. Where I'd attended Super Kids camp as a kid. Where I'd worked right after college.

On one of the hottest days of the year, I walked the quad with a cooler backpack full of cold drinks. I stood at booths at the student org fair. I walked into the dean's office. The president's office. I created business cards with QR codes and pitched my idea to complete strangers—red-faced, awkward, asking for what I needed.

The voting system was confusing. Pure madness. So I didn't just pitch and hand out drinks—I stood there, helping people figure out the registration in real time. That was the number-one complaint: "*This voting is so annoying.*" And they were right. But they still showed up for me. Because they couldn't scroll past me. Because I was a real person asking for what I needed. Because when you show up in person and say, "*I'm trying to help people like you, and I need your help to do it,*" something shifts.

The coaches said, "*Be brave. Push through the awkward. Share your message.*" But what they meant was: "*Perform online.*" That didn't feel like courage. It felt like exposure. Like being visible before I was ready. Like saying things before I even knew if I believed them. I posted what I thought would land—what people wanted, what would perform—and something felt off.

It all felt hollow. Like I wasn't helping, or that I was shaping myself to fit the response. I wasn't sharing. I was presenting.

But in person? I saw humans' faces, all those *aha* moments and micro-expressions. I felt the feedback in real time, as a true exchange of energy. And people were excited, because someone showed up in person.

In my years at Uber, I'd been visiting campuses and giving personal development workshops on burnout, imposter syndrome, how to ace the internship. I'd work with student orgs to decide the topic. No PR. No social campaigns. Just real people in a room. And then I'd show up to an evening-with-industry dinner with the Society of Women Engineers at UC Berkeley, and students would approach me. *"I know you don't remember me, but I met you two years ago, and your imposter syndrome workshop is why I landed my job at Amazon."*

I was a celebrity, of sorts— not online, but to the people whose lives I'd touched.

I got the votes and managed to secure the SXSW EDU speaking spot. All by showing people, in person, what I wanted to build. Through the social media coach, the book writing coach, the scoff from the faculty member, I kept listening to myself. And I proved something I needed to know: *You can do it another way.*

Maybe it's harder. Maybe you have to walk the quad, red-faced and awkward, making individual asks instead of broadcasting to thousands. But you can activate a community, change lives, make real impact—without an online presence.

I wasn't a failed influencer. I was someone who refused to turn my nervous system into a content engine before I had the language, protection, or stability to do so. I rejected unregulated visibility before I could name why. And now, having paused, reflected, and built the tools, I can show up online in a way that feels like service, not performance. Not from the wound, but from the lens.

I still think about those students, the captain of the intramural volleyball team and the young woman working the desk at the Center for the Study of the Holocaust and Genocide. The ones who couldn't scroll past me. The ones who took time out of their day on the hottest afternoon of the year to believe in something, simply because another human being asked. That's the kind of influence that lasts.

When we get away from the algorithms and metrics, we start to see real life again.

PROOF OVER PERMISSION

I've applied to speak at multiple TEDx events and got the kind of responses that sound thoughtful but land hard. Too many talks already existed in this space. My idea wasn't impactful or novel enough for the stage.

TEDx said no. Other rooms said yes.

The same day as one of the rejections, a student organizer posted they were hoping to bring in Olympic gold medalist Alyssa Liu. It stung. Quietly, but fully. The kind of moment where you recognize the level, the bar—what the stage is optimizing for.

Also, it made sense. She is incredible.

That moment didn't make me question the work. It made me panic. Not because I needed the stage, but because if this topic could be dismissed as "not novel enough," it meant the problem had done exactly what it does best.

It had become invisible by becoming so common, we stopped seeing it.

The attention economy doesn't announce itself. It just becomes the water we swim in. The problem wasn't that this topic wasn't new. The problem was that it had become so ingrained in our daily lives that we had lost the ability to recognize it as a problem at all.

That terrified me. And it made me more resolute.

I'd already proven I could show up in person when it mattered. The votes came. The speaking spot came. And I had living proof.

The students living inside the problem said it was everywhere. One of the biggest issues of our time. Maybe the biggest.

Weeks before speaking at SXSW EDU, Sean's father passed away. I decided to shorten my trip and flew from San Francisco to Austin for one night, just for the talk. I landed, ordered Torchy's Tacos to the Tommie Hotel, and slept for fifteen hours. Grief is its own kind of tired.

I wasn't as prepared as I wanted to be. I knew it.

But I kept thinking about Alyssa Liu—not the gold medals, not the strange coincidence of her name surfacing the same day the last TEDx rejection did. But her mentality. How she shows up to be there, not to prove something. How the outcome was never really the point.

That's the energy I walked in with, which was a good thing, because the slides didn't work. The presenter screen didn't load. For twenty, maybe thirty minutes, multiple people tried to make the tech work.

Nobody could.

I let it go. Relaxed into the room. Stopped trying to manage every variable and focused on the people in front of me—no notes, just conviction for the message.

Once I stopped trying to get it right, nothing was wrong.

A few weeks later, I spoke at the annual URx conference in Las Vegas. I was back in a familiar world—the recruiting and talent community where I'd spent most of my career. The room got it immediately. The idea wasn't too niche. It wasn't too soft. It just wasn't TED.

Afterward, talent professionals came up to me, saying something had shifted. Not in how they thought about their programs—in how they thought about the people inside them. One told me she'd stopped diagnosing her interns as unmotivated and started asking what she was asking their attention to survive.

They weren't there for a wellness talk. They were there for a talent strategy conversation. Somewhere in the middle of it, the two turned out to be the same thing.

That landed differently than I expected.

We didn't lose willpower.

We lost boundaries.

And once I saw that, I couldn't stop seeing it.

Red would have been posting about the rejection. Performing resilience before I'd processed it. Turning the "no" into content.

Yellow would have been letting the gatekeepers' verdict become my own measure. Scaling back quietly. Waiting for permission.

Green was flying into SXSW EDU after my partner's father passed away. One night, grief in my chest, no notes, slides that never loaded. There was a moment when I could feel myself reaching—for control, for approval, for it to land the right way. And then I didn't. Not because I was sure. Because I didn't need it to go any particular way.

QUIET POWER

I didn't major in philosophy. But for a few years, I lived inside it. Working at UC Santa Cruz, I was surrounded by graduate students and faculty who thought out loud for a living. I was an adviser, someone adjacent to the ideas. Or so I thought.

There was a bench at Cowell College where I used to sit at lunch. The college tiered down the hillside, redwood trees rising all around and Monterey Bay stretching before me. I was twenty-four, dressed in professional clothes I'd chosen carefully to seem older than I was, thinking about Senior Advising Week and graduation deadlines and whether anyone in the room had noticed I was the youngest person there.

That moment, I was just letting the Bay do what the Bay does. Quiet the noise. Make the morning feel smaller than it had.

Sitting between the redwoods and the water, with enough stillness for an idea to take hold, I suddenly appreciated the full significance of something I'd heard recently.

That's what stillness does. It makes room.

Power isn't declared; it's demonstrated. Action, not intention, is what reveals who we are.

It was political philosopher Hannah Arendt's idea. I just didn't know it yet.

We've been trained to believe that impact is loud. If something mattered, it would trend. If it worked, we would see it everywhere. If it were powerful, someone would be talking about it. Visibility has become our proxy for value, noise our shorthand for influence.

Yet some of the most consequential shifts of the last decade didn't arrive with a campaign or an announcement. They arrived quietly, after periods of erasure, misrepresentation, and collapse, through people who stopped explaining themselves and let their actions do the talking.

Arendt spent her life studying how power moves, not how it's marketed or declared.

When Olivia Dean won her Grammy, she did what almost no one at the peak of a career-defining moment thinks to do. She logged off. No victory lap on Instagram. No acceptance speech reposts. No carefully lit content from the night that changed everything.

Just the win, held privately, lived fully, shared with the people who were in the room. In a culture that treats visibility as validation and silence as surrender, she chose the opposite—not because she was afraid of the spotlight, but because she understood something most people learn too late. The moment you perform your most meaningful experiences for an audience, you stop fully living them.

Olivia won the Grammy. Then she went home.

Taylor Swift lived inside that logic longer than almost anyone. Hyper-visible, hyper-commented on, profitable for an industry that built empires on her voice while slowly stripping her of control over it. She was recorded without consent. Publicly framed as manipulative. Edited into a narrative that cast her as dishonest. Then she watched as the masters she'd written as a teenager, the work which had built an empire, were sold out from under her with the blessing of an industry that treated her authorship as expendable.

When she protested, she was called "dramatic." When she explained, she was called "calculating." When she showed emotion, it became evidence against her.

This is how erasure works in public life: You're invited to speak just long enough to be discredited.

She rerecorded her albums, a structural correction that rewrote the rules of ownership across the music industry. She rerecorded songs she'd written at sixteen, note for note, to make them legally hers again. It was patient, unflashy work, executed over years. People didn't just cheer. The conversations shifted. Power shifted. What looked like silence was actually precision.

There's a parallel insight in Robert Greene's *The 48 Laws of Power,* which examines how power is preserved, lost, and reclaimed across history. Greene is often misread as cynical, but at the core of his message lives an uncomfortable truth: The loudest moves invite resistance, while the quiet ones redraw the map before anyone realizes what's happened.

Visibility attracts resistance. Explanation creates leverage for others. Power consolidates best when it's underestimated.

The Eras Tour wasn't a pivot back to noise. It was the culmination of years of quiet power finally made undeniable. After rebuilding ownership, song by song, Taylor Swift stepped onto the largest stage of her career—not to ask for recognition, but to demonstrate it. The tour wasn't just a concert series; it was a retrospective of reclaimed identity. Every era, on her terms. Every song, owned. Every night, evidence.

This wasn't loudness as desperation. It was loudness as sovereignty.

The scale mattered, because the foundation was already secure. The spectacle worked because the work had been done. What the world witnessed wasn't a comeback, but a culmination—the visible proof of a woman who had survived erasure, collapse, and silence, only to return a structurally untouchable powerhouse.

I recognize this pattern personally. There was a point where I thought momentum had to be visible to be real. Posting what I was building, sharing what I was thinking, trying to prove I was moving forward in real time, yet still feeling like I was falling behind.

Some of the most meaningful outcomes in my life didn't come from broadcasting my intentions on LinkedIn. They came from stepping back, doing the work quietly, and letting results speak where words would have thinned them.

The work that changed things didn't happen online. It happened off- screen.

Weekends spent building workshops. A full year in a mastermind, learning the craft of speaking instead of performing it. Saying yes to the reps, over and over, without needing them to be seen.

Then things started to move.

I was leading campus workshops in Berkeley, Michigan, and Toronto. Sitting across from university presidents and deans. Walking into USC alongside the CEO of Uber. Speaking at South by Southwest EDU, getting invited into rooms I hadn't posted my way into.

What mattered most, of course, was what happened inside those rooms—students who walked in unsure of themselves, only to leave with a wholly different vision of the future. The messages I received weeks later saying something clicked, something shifted, something changed. Moments I was never in the room for, but somehow helped create.

One student said something that stayed with me: "*Your legacy lives on in each one of us.*"

None of that came from making it about me. It came from stepping back, focusing on the work, and letting the impact carry further than I ever could have on my own.

There was even a point when my role was eliminated. On paper, it looked like what I had built didn't exist. But the work was still out there, in the students, in the programs, in the rooms I had already left. That's when it became clear: I hadn't been working for recognition. I had been working for repetition. For impact. For something that would outlast me.

Quiet power doesn't mean disappearing forever. It means knowing when explanation weakens you, and when the strongest move is to stop narrating and start *acting*. Taylor Swift didn't reclaim her power by convincing people she deserved it. She reclaimed it by building something no one could take from her, and then, only then, letting the world see it.

That's the shift. Not silence as punishment. But discernment, the ability to tell the difference between speaking because it's expected and acting because it's necessary. In a world addicted to noise, the most radical thing you can do is let your work speak before you do.

I didn't fully understand what that looked like until I saw it up close.

Gab Bosche ran the whole thing. Long red hair, sparkly pink pantsuits, high heels—a former pageant queen turned CEO of The Purpose Company. When she walks into a room, people notice.

I'd met her before. But after three days inside a forty-person mastermind in Arizona—learning how to turn your purpose into something that helps people—I found myself talking to her, and something felt different. I expected it to be quick. Polite. The kind of interaction that moves along because there are other people waiting.

Instead, she stopped. Looked at me. Fully at me. Like I was the only conversation happening anywhere. In a room of forty people, with every reason to be somewhere else, she stayed with me. Her attention wasn't scattered across competing priorities. It was directed. Chosen. Given freely. The experience felt rare because it has become rare.

And the more I thought about it, the more it made me think about my grandfather.

He was a prop maker for the studios. He built Disneyland sets and movie sets, including *The Orca*—the boat from *Jaws*. He built worlds for a living. But they were worlds people chose to enter. You planned your trip. You bought your ticket. Then, eventually, you went home.

Somewhere between his generation and mine, that boundary disappeared. The worlds stopped waiting for us to arrive. They started following us home.

He built exits into everything he made.

We forgot that was an option.

Looking back, I think that's why those three moments stayed with me. The bench at Cowell. The CEO in Arizona. My grandfather's worlds.

None of them was trying to command attention.

They simply knew where to place it.

That's not a power strategy. That's an attention practice. And somewhere along the way, I stopped being able to tell the difference between the two.

YOUR IMPACT DIAL

How you show up matters more than you think—not just to others, but to you.

Red: The work is performing instead of landing. You post about it before you do it. You measure whether it mattered by how it was received. You finish something and immediately check to see if anyone noticed, instead of sitting with whether it was real. The gap between what you put out and what you feel is widening.

Yellow: You're showing up, but still listening for the response. You do the work. You're in the room. But part of you is still watching how it lands. You care more about whether it reached people than whether it was true. You're close. The awareness is there, but the full release isn't yet.

Green: You're in it for what it actually does. You show up in rooms no one is filming. You say the true thing instead of the safe thing. You let the work travel further than you can see, and you trust that it does. Impact has stopped feeling like something you need to witness. You just keep going.

Ask yourself: Which color describes how you've been showing up lately? Not your best moment. Your pattern.

WAYS TO MAKE IT COUNT

Impact doesn't require an audience. Most of it happens in rooms when no one is watching. In conversations that will never be documented. In the moment you stayed when leaving would have been easier.

You won't always know when something landed. Often, you won't find out. The student who needed to hear it won't always tell you. The room that shifted won't always announce it. That's not a failure of feedback. That's how real impact moves. Quietly. Further than you can see.

The question isn't how to be seen. It's whether what you're doing is actually true. Whether you're in the room or performing being in the room. Whether you showed up for the moment or for what the moment would look like.

The cooler backpack. The hottest day of the year. Red-faced and awkward, asking complete strangers for help.

That's what it looks like. Not glamorous. Not optimized. Just real. And the ones who couldn't scroll past you—they remember.

Not because an algorithm told them to.

Because you were there.

part iii

when not to use tech

SILENCE AS MEDICINE

Think of the last time you experienced beauty without reaching for your phone: the dinner where conversation deepened because no one documented it, the sunset that held your full attention, the walk where you could just *be,* instead of perform. Those moments stay with us precisely because they remain unposted.

Why? We don't remember the moments we captured. We remember the moments we surrendered to. So let me ask you this: *When was the last time you let a moment live only in your memory?* Portia asked the same question in Sicily. She just didn't have an answer yet. That's why it landed the way it did.

I made a decision early in my corporate career that I never talked about. I had two phones. One was sage green: mine, the newest iPhone. The other was coral red: corporate standard issue. The company offered fifty dollars a month to use your personal phone for work. I turned it down.

What I kept instead was harder to put a price on. Every Friday, when I put the coral red phone in my desk drawer, I felt something I can only describe as taking off pantyhose after a long day. The tension: gone. The relaxation: immediate. The relief: otherworldly. Two days when the only things that could reach me were the ones I had *chosen* to let reach me.

Nobody knew I was doing this. It was a quiet decision that my time was mine on the weekends, and a corporate phone was the cleanest method to keep it that way. I'd rather carry two devices all week than carry work into my weekend, on the only screen that was supposed to be mine.

After that, I carried that boundary through every subsequent job. Just as the thing I did that kept me functional.

Then the pandemic arrived, and my corporate phone went into the cabinet next to the extra paper and the camera gear. The things I didn't use every day but needed access to. I was setting up my home studio, and I put it there without thinking much about it. Weeks passed. Then months. Nobody noticed. Not my team. Not my manager. Not the people for whom I was performing at a high level every single day, from a desk in my own home. If I were truly working from home, why would I need another device? Another thing to check. Another thing to pull my attention away from the work I was there to do.

Eventually, I turned it into the IT desk. I left the old number on my directory page. Just in case. That's when it hit me. The boundary I thought I needed wasn't being enforced by the device. It was being enforced by *me*. That was the most radical thing I ever did in corporate. I never powered it back on. And somewhere along the way, I forgot I had turned it off.

There was a guy I used to work with in San Francisco who started eating his lunch outside. Not in a park, exactly, more like one of those concrete pockets near the Chase Center—a tech-first arena designed with Accenture and the home of the Golden State Warriors, flanked by Uber's corporate offices, anchored by an open quad with a larger-than-life screen where they often hosted community and pregame events. It's the kind of place where the fan experience has been so thoroughly engineered that even the air outside feels sponsored. The kind of place where "getting fresh air" means standing between a stadium and corporate buildings, convincing yourself that sunlight on your face is enough.

According to him, the first few minutes felt wrong. Like he was wasting time, like he should've been catching up on something. His hand kept reaching for his phone. Unlock, lock, set it back down.

Instead, he wound up watching a pigeon for longer than he meant to—one of those San Francisco pigeons that's completely unbothered, like it pays premium rent and has nowhere urgent to be. He listened to people walking by: startup pitches mid-sentence, someone pacing on a call like the sidewalk was their office, the low hum of a city that never really logs off.

There, in the middle of it all, he realized he couldn't remember the last time he'd sat without doing something else at the same time. By the time he went back inside, something had quietly reset. He couldn't explain it, couldn't point to what changed. He just told me, "I felt calmer." So he did it again the next day. Same bench. Same nothing. It became the best part of his day.

An hour north, amid Sonoma County's rolling hills and open spaces, the same thing was playing out rather differently. A friend told me about her son's Saturday Little League game she almost missed, not because she wasn't there, but because she wasn't *really* there. Sidelines full of parents in athleisure and sunglasses, iced coffees in hand, phones out. Group chats open. Half-reading emails that still felt urgent, even on a Saturday morning next to a baseball field.

She was one of them. Her son was on the field and she was somewhere else entirely. Then he scored. She, looked up a second too late, just in time to see everyone else react. The cheering, kids piling on, her son glancing toward the sideline.

She put her phone in her bag and didn't take it out again. Watched the rest of the game with both eyes. She noticed the way he ran, the way he looked back at her after a good play, the small things that wouldn't make it into any highlight reel. By the time they walked to the car together, she felt like she'd actually been there.

Later, he asked, "Did you see my hit?"

This time, she had.

Most of us aren't absent from our lives all at once. Just a little at a time.

In a world designed to keep us restless, silence has become a radical act of repair. We pay for retreats to learn things our grandparents got for free, while worshiping Wi-Fi and worrying about going off the grid—signs we're in desperate need of a pause. But silence isn't just an escape from noise. It's a return to oneself. What the world calls luxury, your body calls home.

That's how fragile our peace has become. One ping and we're in pieces. Attention isn't infinite; it's energy. Silence lightens the mind's cognitive load. It allows our memory to reset, with pockets of calm nudging the body from fight-or-flight to rest-and-digest. Just as your body heals with rest, your mind repairs itself in silence. And have you ever noticed how your shoulders drop when you exhale? That's because the body often finds stillness before the mind does.

Start somewhere small—one app, one window, one honest conversation with someone who'll hold you to it. As author and researcher Anne Lamott says, almost everything will work again if you unplug it for a few minutes, including you.

Silence starts as a feeling, but it becomes sustainable through design. Mine started with a single rule: no phone in bed. It changed my routine, giving space to breathe before the day began. The language you use with yourself sets the tone for everything that follows—the quieter and kinder it gets, the easier the rest becomes.

You can't heal what you don't notice. So pay attention to the tiny shifts that tell you you're coming back to yourself, the few minutes before your first screen, the meals you eat without reaching for your phone, the pauses that no longer feel like punishment. Each one is proof that stillness is working. You're not disconnecting from life. You're reconnecting to it.

The goal was never to escape discomfort. It was to finally hear what it's been trying to say.

Because once you do, something changes. You stop reaching as often. You notice more. You feel less behind.

And slowly, quietly, your life starts to feel like yours again.

ACCESS DENIED

Every app is built on one assumption: that we're always available. Even when we're resting, our digital lives hum quietly in the background. Those constant nudges train our nervous systems to believe we're never off-duty. Research shows 75 percent of Americans check their phones within five minutes of receiving an alert. I remember the first time I turned off my notifications—not just silencing them, but truly *off*. My phone sat there like a quiet caged animal, waiting for a command that never came. The stillness was unnerving, my body trained to flinch every time it lit up.

I measured my worth in vibrations, but after a few days, my brain stopped bracing for the next ping. I started finishing thoughts, sentences, even meals. It wasn't about discipline. It was about relief. That's when I realized silence wasn't empty. It was restorative. It didn't feel like a punishment or some productivity hack. It felt like finally exhaling after years of holding my breath underwater. The quiet didn't demand anything from me. It didn't ask for a reply or offer a quick hit of validation. It just existed. Soft. Steady. Enough.

For the first time in a long time, I wasn't reacting to the world. I was *with* it. I could hear my own thoughts again, uncluttered and uncurated. The kind that don't fit neatly into captions or text bubbles. The kind that comes slowly, the way truth usually does.

Silence isn't the absence of connection. It's the space that makes real connection possible.

We think technology connects us, but sometimes it's our disconnection that brings us back to life. We've been tricked into believing that being reachable makes us reliable, when really, more access often means more anxiety, not more connection. Every DM, Slack ping, and read receipt has become a new form of emotional labor, a digital tax on presence.

My twenty-year-old self wasn't far off. All those times I avoided texts or felt that sudden rush of dread after a notification, it wasn't coldness. It was anxiety-avoidant attachment disguised as digital boundaries.

We don't just bring our phones into relationships. We bring our attachment styles too. If you lean avoidant, you ignore texts, ghost group chats, and thrive in Do Not Disturb—the devices become the perfect escape hatch, a way to stay close enough to feel connected and far enough to feel safe. If you lean anxious, you over-text, overthink every delay, check Last Seen like it's a vital sign—devices become a slot machine for validation, always promising connection, rarely delivering calm. And if you're secure, you reply with intention and log off without guilt, because your worth was never in the notification to begin with.

Our screens amplify who we already are.

Technology doesn't create these patterns; it simply reflects our wiring back to us in high definition. But awareness changes everything. The moment you catch yourself reaching, refreshing, checking, scrolling—that's the moment you start to reclaim choice. Awareness isn't loud or dramatic. It's quiet power, the pause between impulse and action. The breath where you remember: *I can choose differently this time.*

When our nervous systems live in "always on" mode, even rest starts to look like withdrawal. We call it "decompressing," but it's not the kind that restores. It's the kind that numbs. "Bed rotting" isn't laziness; it's a symptom of overstimulation. The body is exhausted, and the brain is still buffering. We call it "self-care," but often it's digital sedation. Our bodies are trying to rest while our minds are wired.

We lie there, phones inches from our faces, chasing comfort through content. We scroll through other people's morning routines while our own dreams collect dust. We tell ourselves we're taking a break, but really we're still performing presence for the algorithm.

Saying "access denied" isn't about pushing the world away. It's about protecting your peace enough to stay open to it. Because boundaries aren't walls. They're doors with intentional keys, and the truth is that the people who respect your silence are the ones who deserve your attention.

Every time you say no to the noise, you say yes to your nervous system, your joy, your wholeness. Denial, in this context, isn't rejection. It's you reclaiming your life, one tap, click, and swipe at a time.

When I finally started reclaiming my attention, it didn't happen all at once. It happened in small denials that felt like relief: turning off one notification, leaving one message unanswered, choosing to rest instead of refreshing.

At first, it felt rebellious. Then it became peaceful. I used to think boundaries were about control, but they're about care. Every time I said no to the noise, I could finally hear myself think again.

Every time you say no to something online, you say yes to something in real life.

THE QUIET FLEX

In a world obsessed with visibility, disappearing is the new superpower. If Taylor Swift showed us what it looks like to reclaim power publicly, actress Emma Watson offers a different blueprint: what it means to reclaim yourself privately.

Before she was Hermione Granger, she was a child stepping onto the set of *Harry Potter and the Sorcerer's Stone,* believing she had found something permanent.

For many of us, Hermione wasn't just a character. She was our girl. The one we waited in line for. Midnight book releases, opening-night premieres, gripping the pages and trying to keep up with her mind. She was the girl with wild hair, the stack of books, her ink-stained fingers always raised in the air because she always had the answer. She was the one who stayed. She was certainty. Loyalty. Identity. We didn't just watch her. We grew up with her.

For Emma Watson, that world was real.

In an interview on Jay Shetty's podcast *On Purpose,* Watson spoke with unusual candor about what those years gave her and what they cost. "I was coming to those sets with an expectation... that the people I worked with were going to be my family."

For a while, they were. Twelve years. A world that grew up with her. A structure that held her identity in place. But when the films ended, so did the illusion of permanence. "I came to work looking for friendship... and that was bone-breakingly painful."

The industry she entered didn't offer belonging. It offered performance. Visibility without protection. Then came the deeper fracture: the split between who she was and who the world expected her to be.

"'Emma Watson' became this avatar," she said. "She felt too heavy to carry." At some point, the question changed. Not what's next, but: *Is this even mine?* "You have the life that looks like the dream," she added. "But are you really happy?"

The answer was no. "If it costs me any part of my peace, it's too expensive."

She didn't disappear from public view because she failed. She disappeared because she refused to keep performing a version of herself that no longer felt true. Fewer roles. Fewer appearances. Less access. More life that wasn't explained, documented, or offered up for consumption. "I didn't want to pretend to be my real life," she said.

In a culture that rewards constant visibility, she chose something else entirely: selective absence. Not retreat. Not irrelevance. Discernment. That's the quiet flex. Choosing yourself before the world decides for you.

There's a reason stepping away feels radical, and it goes deeper than social media. Philosopher Michel Foucault argued that modern power doesn't just operate through force—it operates through observation. Through the feeling of being seen. The expectation that you are always visible, always accountable to an audience.

Over time, you start watching yourself. Editing yourself. Performing without being asked. What looks like expression becomes anticipation. What looks like connection becomes compliance. Social media didn't create this dynamic. It scaled it. It turned everyday life into something that feels like it should be documented, explained, and understood by others in real time. Not because anyone explicitly asked you to, but because the system rewards those who do.

The cost is subtle. You stop asking what you want to do, and start asking what would look good, what would land, what would be worth sharing. You don't just live your life. You edit it.

I didn't have a global stage or a franchise behind me. But I recognized the same pattern in my own life. After my sabbatical in Tulum, I chose to go dark on social media. It was simple: I wanted space to write *Reclaim*. I was waiting to share intentionally, not reactively—until I was aligned, not anxious. Until my becoming felt mine, not crowdsourced.

It gave me space to build something new without having to explain it yet. When layoffs finally came for me, I wasn't caught off guard—I had already been quietly building something else. The time off gave me permission to chase my dreams at a time when stability was only available to those who'd built it for themselves.

I got to play. To get into flow. To be creative without the pressure to perform. To become someone new without carrying the projections of a world I was outgrowing.

In the quiet, I finally heard the parts of myself I'd muted for years. The parts that wanted to create, to speak, to write boldly, to try things without needing to be instantly excellent. I spoke at Berkeley and Uber and SXSW EDU without documenting it. I moved into an apartment on the water and chose presence over content. I let myself become messy, curious, and unfiltered—and I kept it mine.

People assume privacy is avoidance. But it's the opposite: Privacy is leverage. Choosing not to be seen—even briefly, even selectively—interrupts that system. Privacy isn't withdrawal. It's agency. It's the decision to experience something before you explain it. To become someone before you present it. To let your life belong to you again.

We're not built to be watched this much or to perform our lives while living them. Creating in private, without that burden or expectation, is how clarity forms, how courage takes root. It's how your voice gets stronger, without external noise diluting it.

So ask yourself: *Where could silence be my next act of power?* Because in a world that rewards noise, choosing quiet might be the most radical thing you do.

THE RIPPLE EFFECT

We talk about digital boundaries as if they're personal projects—habits we build in private, choices we make for our own sanity. But every moment you choose to look up, someone else feels it. Every time you resist the pull of the screen, you shift the atmosphere in the room just enough that someone else can breathe again.

I've been in rooms where every single person was on their phone. Not because anything urgent was happening, but because no one wanted to be the only one not checking. The silence wasn't peaceful—it was brittle. We were together but alone, each of us waiting for someone to go first, and no one did. The longer it went on, the more normal it felt. That's how culture shifts, through the tiny surrenders we stop noticing.

I've also watched the opposite happen. A dinner party where someone—without announcement or ceremony—slipped their phone into their bag and set it down under the table. That's it. Just one person deciding the room was worth more than their screen. Within minutes, the rest of us followed. Permission had been granted. Suddenly, we were leaning in closer, laughing louder, and staying an extra hour no one had planned for. One person's choice created the conditions for everyone else's. That's how ripples work, through a quiet demonstration that another way is possible.

Cultural conditioning doesn't begin with institutions or policies. It starts in micro-moments: the glance you return instead of the alert you check, the silence you allow instead of filling it, the way your body signals, "I'm here," when everyone else has forgotten how.

Attention is contagious. When you model it, you give people permission to remember they have that choice as well. This is why being present outlives notifications. No one remembers the emails you answered in record time, or the DM you responded to within seconds. But they do remember how you made them feel seen, held, unhurried. They remember the rare gift of someone who wasn't half anywhere, but fully here. Your example teaches more than your words ever will. Your presence today teaches presence tomorrow.

Your power lives there, in the small, unglamorous moment when you choose yourself over the algorithm. Where you prove to your own nervous system: *I can survive without constant input. I can be here, unmediated and whole.*

When you do, you're not just changing a habit. You're teaching everyone watching what connection can look like again, whether it's your child who glances up to see if you're looking back, or the coworker who mirrors your pause before opening Slack, or the stranger who pockets their phone because your stillness reminds them they can too.

But when you don't go first, you're also teaching something. You're signaling that the screen is worth more than the room. That busyness is more important than belonging, that no one here—including you—is worth the full weight of your attention. This is how we reclaim not just our attention, but our lives. The daily, radical decision to be where you are. Fully. Without apology. Without escape.

Presence is the only currency that compounds. Every time you choose it, you make it easier for the next person to choose it too. Every time you look up, you give someone else permission to do the same.

The question, then, isn't just what kind of ripples you're sending out. It's this: What world are you building with your attention? When you look up, you're not just reclaiming your attention. You're reminding the world how to be human again.

WE'RE ALL IN THIS TOGETHER

Whether you're a creator, a CEO, a parent, a student, a techie, or someone just trying to get through the week without drowning in notifications, we're all learning to survive the same attention economy. We're all navigating the same digital pressures, the same overstimulation, the same algorithmic pull on our nervous systems.

And that's where the real work begins. This chapter isn't just a warm-and-fuzzy reminder of unity—it's a wake-up call. Your digital habits don't live in a vacuum. They ripple outward and influence people you will never meet. Whether we like it or not, we're setting the standard for what the next generation will consider "normal."

Our tech choices aren't just personal; they're cultural, communal, and shape the future we're all going to live in. The shift begins not in some dramatic digital detox or overnight transformation, but in the smallest, most human moments: conversations.

The moment we start talking about our digital lives out loud—the habits we're proud of, the ones we're ashamed of, the places we feel addicted, the things we wish we could change—we begin to change. The silence breaks. The shame dissolves. Real connections flower. Suddenly, what felt like a private struggle becomes a shared human experience.

That's the part no one tells you: Digital healing gets more powerful the moment it leaves your head and enters the room. Tell one person the truth about how your phone makes you feel. Tell them what you're working on, what you're trying to reclaim, what part of your digital life feels a little too loud or a little too lonely. Ask them what feels hard for them too. Let the conversation be imperfect. Let it be human.

The moment two people speak honestly about their digital lives, a tiny movement forms between them. A spark. One person choosing presence gives someone else permission. One boundary makes it easier for someone else to set their own. One honest sentence can shift an entire room. One room can shift a workplace. One workplace can shift a culture.

Sometimes, one person shifts the world.

In front of the entire globe, on the biggest athletic stage imaginable at the Tokyo Olympics, Simone Biles stepped back and said, "We have to protect our mind and our body, rather than just go out there and do what the world wants us to do."

People didn't know how to process this, because we aren't used to seeing the best in the world choose humanity over performance, or choose truth over pressure.

For Biles, the experience was a terrifying disconnect between her mind and her body known as the "twisties." She described it as waking up one day and suddenly having no idea how to drive the car you've driven every day of your life, losing all control over your limbs while moving at high speeds in midair. During her training and the early stages of the competition, she felt like she was fighting her body and her mind just to perform her skills. When she finally took the runway for the vault, she had no idea what her body would do once she hit the table, saluting the judges while praying simply to land on her feet.

The moment she landed, her first thought wasn't about her physical safety, but about the crushing weight of public expectation. "America hates me. The world is going to hate me," she recalled thinking, fearing she would be banned from the country for not bringing home a gold medal. Despite that fear, she walked off the mat and told her coach she was done—feeling like she had used up the last of whatever reserves she had as an athlete. She realized that her pride wasn't worth the risk of a catastrophic injury that would also prevent her team from even being able to contend for a medal.

By stepping back, Biles transformed her role entirely. She was no longer the one expected to carry everything, but the one cheering loudest for the people she loved. She chose to protect herself rather than perform until she broke. That moment did more than shift sports culture. It shifted digital culture too. It reminded us that behind every comment section and every headline is a real person with a real nervous system, trying to hold it all together.

When someone with her level of visibility publicly honors their humanity, it gives the rest of us permission to honor ours in private. Biles didn't just protect her mental health. She cracked something open for all of us. She made it clear that our worth is not found in our output, our productivity, or our performance—it is found in our ability to stay human in a world that constantly asks us not to be.

Everywhere you want to be. Build for Everyone. Power of the Platform. I was the first in my family to sit in rooms like that. Of course, I believed every word. They were honest. They were all-consuming. And now they're just what we call life. This book is about remembering that you get to call it something else.

I didn't set out to write this book. I set out to figure something out.

It started on a dock in the San Juan Islands, watching kids arrive clutching their last moments of connectivity and leave weeks later having forgotten they needed it. It continued in a stucco studio across from the boardwalk at sunset, where someone handed me a warning I wouldn't understand for a decade.

It showed up in rooms at Berkeley and Michigan and SXSW EDU, where I stopped documenting and started being present. Where I stopped feeling guilty for not performing and started noticing the impact was larger than impressions. Where I understood for the first time that purpose doesn't lack likes. That life-changing moments don't require reels or reach.

And it lives in the person who found a way to reach me through every screen I put between us. Who made a sound instead of an argument.

I was always living this book. I just didn't know it until I started writing it.

ACKNOWLEDGMENTS

To the students who sat across from me, wondering if what they were feeling was normal, to the colleagues who confessed they couldn't focus anymore, and to the friends who quietly admitted they felt like they were disappearing: Thank you. Your stories shaped these pages long before I ever sat down to write them.

To my coaches and mentors, thank you for challenging me to think bigger than what felt comfortable. When self-doubt crept in, you reminded me what I was capable of. Your questions sharpened my thinking, your encouragement steadied me, and your belief in this work helped carry it from an idea to a finished book.

To my editorial team, proofreaders, designers, and publishing partners, thank you for helping bring this book to life. Every question, edit, and design decision made these pages clearer, stronger, and more impactful. I am deeply grateful for your expertise and care.

To my PR and marketing team, thank you for helping bring this message beyond the page. Your work has helped create opportunities to share these ideas with readers, students, and audiences seeking a healthier relationship with technology and attention.

To my mom, thank you for telling me my stories were worth telling long before I believed it myself. You paid for tutors, you listened to every idea, and you always said this was a book worth writing. You were right.

To my partner Sean, thank you for every "zz-zz" that brought me back to the present, and for giving me the space to finish this book. Many of the lessons in these pages began with moments we experienced together.

And finally, to Ziggy, my loyal writing companion. Thank you for spending countless hours by my side throughout the writing of this book. Some of my best ideas came during our walks along the bay and the quiet drives to the redwoods that gave me space to think.

You always seemed to know when I needed a break from my screen. When the words weren't coming, you got me outside. When I was stuck in my head, you reminded me to be present. Through every draft, edit, and rewrite, you never left my side.

He never read a word of it. He didn't need to. He just kept showing up—which, as it turns out, is the whole point.

ABOUT THE AUTHOR

Heather Henderson is the author of *Reclaim: How to Stop Scrolling Through Your Life and Start Living It.* A former Big Tech insider and university recruiter, she helps people understand how technology shapes their attention and how to reclaim the ability to choose what matters most.

A first-generation college student, Henderson grew up on a college campus where her mother worked as a staff member. She began her career as an academic advisor at the University of California, Santa Cruz. She later spent more than a decade recruiting talent for Visa, Accenture, Google, and Uber, including the engineers who helped build many of the digital products people use every day. Her work gave her a rare perspective on both sides of the screen: the people designing technology and the people adapting their lives to it. Over time, she saw a growing pattern among ambitious students and professionals: achievement accompanied by distraction, exhaustion, and disconnection.

In *Reclaim,* Henderson challenges the idea that people are failing simply because they cannot put down their phones. Instead, she asks readers to consider a more revealing question: *Did I choose this, or was it chosen for me?*

Through her writing and speaking, she explores attention, digital habits, presence, and the quiet ways technology influences human behavior. Henderson speaks at universities, conferences, and organizations, helping audiences build healthier relationships with technology and thrive in the attention economy.

She lives in the San Francisco Bay Area with her partner and their Boston Terrier, Ziggy. Learn more at iamheatherh.com.

www.ingramcontent.com/pod-product-compliance
Lightning Source LLC
LaVergne TN
LVHW100727061126
851857LV00011B/430
9798996161911